REMEMBERING BEETHOVEN

Beethoven's silhouette at age 16

REMEMBERING BEETHOVEN

The Biographical Notes of
Franz Wegeler and Ferdinand Ries

Foreword by Christopher Hogwood
Introduction by Eva Badura-Skoda

ANDRE DEUTSCH

Translated from the German
Biographische Notizen über Ludwig van Beethoven (1838, 1845)
by Frederick Noonan

Notes by Dr. Alfred C. Kalischer
from his edition of the text (2nd edition, Berlin, 1906)
translated by Frederick Bauman and Tim Clark

Illustrations reproduced through the courtesy and with permission
of the sources cited in the list of Illustrations.

Book design by M. Esterman

First published in Great Britain 1988 by
André Deutsch Limited
105-106 Great Russell Street London WC1B 3LJ

ISBN 0 233 98285 X

Printed in Great Britain by
St Edmundsbury Press, Bury St Edmunds, Suffolk

Contents

List of Illustrations vi

Foreword by Christopher Hogwood. ix

Introduction by Eva Badura-Skoda xi

Part I by Franz Gerhard Wegeler (1838). 1

Part II by Ferdinand Ries (1838) 63

Supplement by Franz Gerhard Wegeler (1845). . . 144

Notes by Alfred C. Kalischer 168

Index 193

Index of Musical Compositions 198

Illustrations

1 Beethoven's silhouette at age 16, by Joseph Neesen, 1786 — frontispiece of the original edition *(Beethoven-Haus, Bonn, H.C. Bodmer Collection)* *frontispiece*

2 Sketch of Beethoven by J.D. Böhm, c. 1820 *(Beethoven-Haus, Bonn)* viii

3 Anton Schindler (1798-1864) *(Bild-Archiv der Österreichischen Nationalbibliothek, Vienna)* xv

4 Autograph letter from Ferdinand Ries to Carl Czerny, 1830 *(Archiv der Gesellschaft der Musikfreunde, Vienna)* xix

5 Franz Gerhard Wegeler (1765-1848) *(Bild-Archiv der Österreichischen Nationalbibliothek, Vienna)* 1

6 Beethoven's birthplace (Bonngasse), pencil drawing by R. Beissel, 1889 *(Bild-Archiv der Österreichischen Nationalbibliothek, Vienna)* 12

7 The von Breuning family, silhouette, 1782 *(Beethoven-Haus, Bonn)* 15

8 The von Breuning family house, Munsterplatz, Bonn, watercolor by M. Frickel *(Stadtarchiv und Wissenschaftliche Stadtbibliothek, Bonn)* 16

9 Christian Gottlob Neefe (1748-1798), engraving by Liebe after a drawing by J.G. Rosenberg *(Archiv der Gesellschaft der Musikfreunde, Vienna)* 18

10 Count Ferdinand von Waldstein (1762-1823), anonymous silhouette from Beethoven's scrapbook *(Bild-Archiv der Österreichischen Nationalbibliothek, Vienna)* 19

11 Stephan von Breuning (1774-1827), portrait by Franz Gerhard von Kugelgen *(Beethoven-Haus, Bonn)* 30

12 Beethoven's portrait (1814) engraved by Blasius Höfel from a pencil drawing by Louis Letronne *(Archiv der Gesellschaft der Musikfreunde, Vienna)* 47

13 Excerpt from Beethoven's letter to Eleonore von Breuning, 2 Nov. 1793 *(from the original German edition)* 54

14 Elector Maximilian Franz (1756-1801), anonymous oil portrait *(Beethoven-Haus, Bonn)* 56

15 Ferdinand Ries (1784-1838), anonymous oil portrait *(Beethoven-Haus, Bonn)* 63

16 Heiligenstadt c. 1821, watercolor by T.D. Raulino *(Historisches Museum der Stadt, Vienna)* 67

17 Nikolaus Simrock (1752-1833), lithograph by Weber *(Stadtarchiv und Wissenschaftliche Stadtbibliothek, Bonn)* 78

18 Prince Karl Lichnowsky (1756-1814) *(Hradec u Opavy, Czechoslovakia)* 92

19 Princess Maria Christiane Lichnowsky (1765-1841)*(Hradec u Opavy, Czechoslovakia)* 92

20 Friedrich Heinrich Himmel (1765-1814) *(Archiv der Gesellschaft der Musikfreunde, Vienna)* 97

21 Archduke Rudolph (1788-1831), engraving by Blasius Höfel after a painting by Adalbert Suchy *(Beethoven-Haus, Bonn)* 99

22 Johann van Beethoven (1740-1792), the composer's father, *(Bild-Archiv der Österreichischen Nationalbibliothek, Vienna)* 110

23 Excerpt from Beethoven's letter to Ferdinand Ries, 20 Jan. 1816 *(from the original German edition)* 122

24 Karl van Beethoven, Beethoven's nephew (1806-1858) *(Bild-Archiv der Österreichischen Nationalbibliothek, Vienna)* 124

25 Excerpt from Beethoven's letter to Ferdinand Ries, 25 April 1823 *(from the original German edition)* 136

26 Nikolaus Johann van Beethoven, Beethoven's youngest brother (1776-1848). Oil painting by Leopold Gross *(Bild-Archiv der Österreichischen Nationalbibliothek, Vienna)* 139

27 Ferdinand Ries, lithograph by L. Lehmann *(Archiv der Gesellschaft der Musikfreunde, Vienna)* 142

28 Musical score of Beethoven's "Die Klage", WoO 113 *(from the original German edition)* 143

29 Beethoven's birthplace (Bonngasse), photograph *(Bild-Archiv der Österreichischen Nationalbibliothek, Vienna)* 147

30 The Fischer house (Rheingasse), Beethoven family residence, drawing *(Bild-Archiv der Österreichischen Nationalbibliothek, Vienna)* 147

31 Miniature portrait of Beethoven on ivory by Christian Hornemann, 1803 *(Beethoven-Haus, Bonn, H.C.Bodmer Collection)* 160

32 Beethoven's study in the Schwarzspanierhaus, lithograph from a sepia drawing by J.N. Hochle, 1827 *(Historisches Museum der Stadt, Vienna)* 165

33 Musical score of Beethoven's "Empfindungen bei Lydiens Untreue", WoO 132 *(from the original German edition)* 166

Sketch of Beethoven by J.D. Böhm, c. 1820

Foreword
by Christopher Hogwood

A significant watershed has been passed recently in the relationship between music and musical biography. We now exist in the post-*Amadeus* period. In earlier times, marked by large volumes of collected correspondence and three-volume studies in depth, the attitude was "rearrange the composer's music if you like, but present the true account of the man." The new age, marked by cinematic afflatus and theatrical fictions, prefers an *Urtext* performance, but rearranges the life.

The change has gone unnoticed by much of the musical public, who were blissfully unaware of lacunae in the documentation of great historical figures, or drowsily assumed the existence of an omniscient college of musicologists monitoring and rationing the flow of propaganda necessary to maintain *The Four Seasons* and Albinoni's *Adagio* at the top of the annual charts.

It will come as something of a shock, therefore, to discover that one of the prime sources of information on Beethoven as seen by a contemporary and colleague has, until now, been unavailable to the English reader. Still more surprising will be the singularity of this most significant human document, produced at a time when it was unprecedented to write of Beethoven with insight, but without the tinge of mythology.

Although extracts from these *Notizen* have appeared in earlier biographies, this new translation of the complete account of Wegeler and Ries carries more immediacy — the immediacy we associate with Beethoven's own conversation books, uncensored by later adulation — and an informality which in itself is a remarkable literary accomplishment.

Ries in particular comes over as a warm and approachable human being, lacking the spite and side of a Schindler, and quite prepared to admit amusedly to his errors in the face of 'modern' music. Like so many of us who dare not admit it so gracefully, he too was fooled the first time he heard the "false entry" of the horn in the *Eroica*. But he also gives us nuggets of psychological insight — Beethoven's improvisations were at their best "especially when he was in a good mood or was irritated" — and pertinent information for the performing musician that can never be found in more portentous tomes — the sparing use of rubato, the effect of a slight rallentando during a crescendo, or the liberating information that Beethoven added octaves to the rondo theme in the C major piano concerto, "to make it more brilliant."

This is Beethoven the Man rather than Beethoven the Myth. To approach the personality behind the music via this unusual memoir can only add to every reader's listening pleasure.

Introduction
by Eva Badura-Skoda

The publication of the *Biographische Notizen über Ludwig van Beethoven* by Franz Gerhard Wegeler and Ferdinand Ries in an English translation is long overdue. Indeed, it is hard to believe that this book has not been published in its entirety for so long. Until now, only excerpts have appeared in the Beethoven books of H. E. Krehbiel and O. G. Sonneck. The value of the recollections of Wegeler is clearly beyond question. Wegeler was Beethoven's close friend during his difficult adolescent years in Bonn and during two of his happy first years in Vienna, a friend in whom Beethoven never lost confidence and who remained in contact with him throughout his life. Of even greater value than the recollections of Wegeler are those of the well-trained musician Ries, Beethoven's only acknowledged pupil besides Archduke Rudolf. Both authors' *Notizen* are comparable in their documentary value to the reports of Haydn's interviewers Griesinger and Dies; and like these they rightly continue to serve as an indispensable source of information for all biographers of the great composer.

Apart from the fact that the accounts of Wegeler and Ries have supplied and will always supply Beethoven biographers with documentary material, these recollections are fascinating reading for every music lover. As A. C. Kalischer pointed out in the foreword to his German edition, Robert

Schumann told a friend immediately after its appearance: "I shall lend you the book; one cannot stop reading it."

Twenty years ago when I started to teach music history at American universities, I was so surprised to discover that the *Notizen* of Wegeler and Ries had never been published in English that I commissioned a translation of it for my own use, not for publication. Besides, others in the field of Beethoven scholarship also were aware of this lack, including English and American colleagues who I thought were in a better position to supply the English speaking world with this urgently needed little book. Since many years have passed with the book still unavailable, I welcomed the invitation of Great Ocean Publishers to write an Introduction to the English edition which they were preparing for publication, especially since it includes the translation of the footnotes of the German Beethoven scholar Kalischer.

The commentaries given in Kalischer's footnotes (indicated by the bold superscripts in the text) help to rectify some memory slips of the two authors. There are some additional minor inaccuracies as the learned reader may notice, but they are of no real importance — diminishing neither the vividness of the picture of Beethoven's personality, nor the trustworthiness of the accounts of these two faithful friends and admirers of Beethoven's genius. The interested reader may be referred to the writings of Stephan Ley (*Wahrheit, Zweifel und Irrtum in der Kunde von Beethoven's Leben*, Wiesbaden 1955), to Clemens Brenneis (*"Das Fischhof-Manuskript: Zur Fruehgeschichte der Beethoven-Biographik,"* in *Zu Beethoven*, ed. by H. Goldschmidt,

Berlin/DDR, 1979), to the valuable edition of nearly 500 letters from and to Ries (*Ferdinand Ries: Briefe und Dokumente*, ed. by Cecil Hill, *Veroeffentlichungen des Stadtarchivs Bonn*, vol. 27, Bonn, 1982) and — last but certainly not least — to the highly relevant article of Alan Tyson in *Nineteenth Century Music* (vol. 7, 3 April 1984), "*Ferdinand Ries (1784-1838): The History of his Contribution to Beethoven Biography.*" In this valuable study, which admirably summarizes the latest research results, Tyson explains for example how it could have happened that Ries erred with regard to the year of his arrival in Vienna (he did not come to Vienna prior to 1801), and that this and some other dating errors were committed *bona fide*. As the prefaces to both parts of the *Notizen* show, the authors' principal aim was to provide accurate data for future studies of Beethoven's life, and they were very concerned indeed about the truthfulness of their reports.

Wegeler can be trusted when he says in his preface: "I feel it necessary to mention that I have set down only what I know for certain." An eminent doctor with a scientific mind, *Rector Magnificus* of the University of Bonn at the age of 29, Wegeler was born in 1765, five years before Beethoven. His relationship to his greatly admired friend in his teenage years reminds one of that between Josef von Spaun and Schubert. After two years of studies in Vienna he returned to the Rhineland, but since he could not pursue his university career because of political reasons he settled in Koblenz and practiced there as a medical doctor, occupying in later years some official positions as well. He married Eleonore von Breuning (who might have been Beethoven's first real love). For more information on Wegeler the interested reader may be referred to the book of Stephan Ley, *Beethoven als Freund der Familie Wegeler-von Breuning*, Bonn, 1927.

In the article on Ries mentioned above, Tyson also explains why a span of ten years passed between Beethoven's death and the publication of the *Notizen* of Wegeler and Ries. This had to do with an assertion of Schindler, Beethoven's "factotum," secretary and self-appointed "friend," who claimed in a letter to Wegeler after Beethoven's and Stephan von Breuning's deaths in 1827 that Beethoven had commissioned him to write his biography together with Stephan von Breuning and Wegeler. Schindler's suggestion was that now, after von Breuning's death, Ries could take over his part in the joint venture of a Beethoven biography. Wegeler, who did not know Schindler well, at first agreed to this proposal. It was Ries who had no real interest in collaborating with Schindler, especially after recognizing that Schindler was less interested in conveying actual facts and impressions than in giving a censored picture of Beethoven according to his own limited understanding of his great master.

Since Schindler in later years made some derogatory, hostile remarks about Ries whom he obviously envied greatly (Ries, unlike Schindler, was a successful composer and performer and highly esteemed as Beethoven's pupil and friend), it seems necessary to say a few words about Schindler.

Anton Schindler was born in 1798 (not 1795 as E. Hueffler claimed) and died in 1864. He wanted the world to believe that he had been Beethoven's "private secretary without pay" almost continuously from the year 1816 (i.e., from the age of 18) on. This assertion is incorporated into most of the modern music dictionaries and encyclopedias when they state that Schindler was "in contact almost daily" with Beethoven for a full ten years. In reality Schindler appears not to have become Beethoven's "unpaid secretary" until 1819 if not later, perhaps even as late as 1822. The greatest number of the

Anton Schindler (1798-1864)

many authenticated errors in the first and second edition of his biography of Beethoven have been found to concern events which happened prior to 1820. From 1822 until May 1823 Schindler lived in the same house as Beethoven. Afterwards, however, their relationship broke off completely, and it was not until December 1826, when Beethoven returned from Gneixendorf to Vienna, already a sick man, that he became reconciled with Schindler and once again entrusted him with secretarial duties. Furthermore Schindler appears to have helped to a considerable extent in caring for Beethoven throughout the serious illness leading up to his death three months later.

Some years ago, when D. W. MacArdle's translation of Schindler's biography of Beethoven appeared in the United States, there were a number of Beethoven scholars who justifiably voiced their concern about the possible harm this new edition might do because the editor had neglected to emphasize sufficiently Schindler's questionable character and his tendency even to forge evidence if he considered it 'necessary' or advisable. This may have been the main reason why he had destroyed some 260 of the approximately 400 conversation notebooks of Beethoven which came into his possession after Beethoven's death. That several entries in the conversation notebooks were indeed forgeries of Schindler, written after 1840, has been proven only rather recently (1978); but the suspicion that Schindler is not trustworthy had been voiced since Nottebohm's times and even earlier; I myself wrote in 1975 in *Notes* (vol. 32, Sept. 1975, p. 47): "Schindler definitely was a neurotic and not always truthful person." Ferdinand Hiller, who as a student of Hummel was allowed to visit Beethoven, gave in his memoirs (p. 46 f.) a lively picture of this man:

> Schindler . . . had brought us to Beethoven, and from then on we saw him rather frequently. The fact that the great master was able to associate with this knight of the most woeful countenance day after day for a number of years, that he did not turn him out, can only be due to the fact that at that time contact with the out-

side world had become a matter of indifference to him and that he had need of an intelligent servant. I do not by any means deny that Schindler had a knowledge of music and certain intellectual abilities — but his personality was as spare as his figure and as dry as his facial features. It is certain that he was of service to Beethoven in many ways — but it is just as certain that no friendship in the world was ever exploited more cleverly and to greater advantage. In later years, on occasions when Schindler was visited by a music lover whom he wanted to honor or please particularly, he would appear wearing an unattractive dressing gown which Beethoven had once worn threadbare, thus presenting, without realizing it, a most accurate picture of his relation to the great man who had merely tolerated him.

Hiller also relates that Beethoven shortly before his death asked his friend Hummel to give a concert for Schindler's benefit, as he himself was unable to do so. And there is indeed no reason to doubt that Beethoven felt indebted to Schindler for the many services he had been unable or unwilling to pay him for, and he may have been very grateful for Schindler's apparently devoted care for him during the days of his final illness. Schindler's biography of Beethoven will always remain an interesting source of information on Beethoven, but far less reliable than the *Notizen* of Beethoven's real friends Wegeler and Ries.

Schindler's unkind remarks about Ferdinand Ries were made in later years and probably caused by Ries's lack of interest in collaborating with Schindler in the biography project. Only after Wegeler had freed himself from any feelings of obligation towards Schindler (he may have even started to doubt Schindler's claim that Beethoven wanted Schindler to write part of his biography) did Ries develop a serious interest in the project.

Years ago and some months before the scholarly world learned about Schindler's forged entries in Beethoven's conversation notebooks, I had commissioned Austria's most gifted and best-known graphologist Robert Muckenschnabel, who had studied 18th and 19th century handwritings in addition to modern ones, to analyze the handwriting of various friends of Beethoven and Schubert, among them Schindler and Ries. Prior to the invention of typewriters, the handwriting of cultivated persons was distinctively personal. Dr. Muckenschnabel, who did not know anything about the writers of the letters he had examined, wrote a shockingly negative character analysis of Schindler (published in my article *"Zum Charakterbild Anton Schindlers," Oesterreichische Musikzeitschrift*, vol. 32, p. 241 f.) which, however, corroborates surprisingly the recently discovered evidence. The examination of Ries's handwriting (based on letters preserved in the Archiv der Gesellschaft der Musikfreunde in Wien and dated Dec. 26, 1825; Nov. 14, 1828; April 25, 1830 and March 6, 1837) resulted in the following character analysis:

> A talented individualist, who has a clear and realistic conception of his own abilities and an enthusiastic love of beauty and noble humanistic goals. He was a reliable, extraordinarily diligent and faithful person, faithful to his friends as well as to himself and his own principles. Sensitive but also easily hurt, grateful and devoted to everyone who had helped him, he was apparently too good-natured and sometimes therefore easily taken advantage of, which may later have been balanced by self-criticism, but

also criticism of others. He suffered perhaps from the fact that he could not do as much for others as he would have liked to, but he had the courage to speak the truth, which may have made him some enemies. Orderly, self-controlled and prudent, he disliked lack of clarity ("das Unklare"). His diligence helped him to fully develop his talent and to become a self-confident, creative and noble human being with high qualities and a cultured style of living.

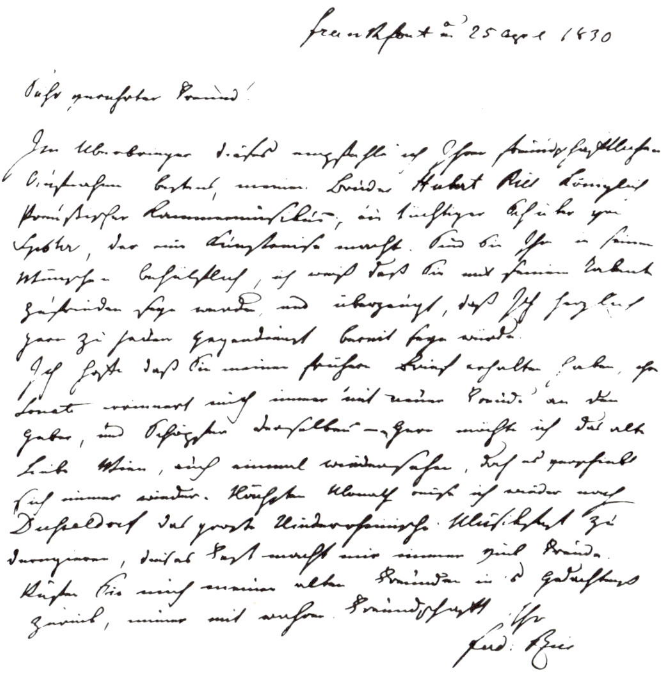

Letter from Ferdinand Ries to Carl Czerny, 1830

No doubt, a graphologist can misjudge handwriting — as no human being can escape the common fate of erring from time to time — but Muckenschnabel's analysis is corroborated by many other sources.

Studies of physiognomy may provide an auxiliary tool, too, for historians who attempt to understand the character qualities of a "witness" from the past; and, indeed, the pictures of Ries and Schindler included in the present volume are "telling" portraits for any perceptive observer.

Ries's father had been a friend of the Beethoven family and, as a violinist in the court orchestra in Bonn, a colleague of Beethoven for many years. Ferdinand Ries learned to admire Beethoven's musical abilities probably even before becoming his student at the age of 17. During the following four years of apprenticeship with Beethoven in Vienna he had unrivalled opportunities for observing Beethoven at work, and through the commissions he was entrusted with such as copying music or proofreading, he gained insight into many of Beethoven's opinions and experiences. It is noteworthy that he and Wegeler made similar observations on certain aspects of Beethoven's character. For instance, Beethoven's hot temper and his easy suspiciousness often led to quarrels and misunderstandings with even his best friends, but would be typically followed by exaggerated feelings of remorse. On the other hand, naïveté was also typical of Beethoven. The inclusion of the priceless story of his childlike faith in Himmel's "news-report" of the invention of a "lantern for the blind" shows that both Wegeler and Ries must have had direct reports that the event had indeed happened, otherwise they would not have included it.

As interesting as the accounts of Beethoven's human reactions are, the real value of the *Notizen* to our knowledge of Beethoven's music lies in those contributions of Ries which allow us an insight into his teacher's musical taste and those few remarks which concern the compositional process and some major works of Beethoven. May the readers of this book share the authors' admiration and love for Beethoven and his music.

Fall 1984

Franz Gerhard Wegeler (1765-1848)

Foreword

Just as these memories of Beethoven's life, jointly collected by Ries and myself, were about to be published, the first report of Ries's illness reached me on the twelfth of January. Then on the following day I was stunned to hear the painful and unexpected news that at one o'clock in the afternoon my fine friend had passed away in the arms of his wife and my son. The shock was especially severe because only a short while before I had spent a week with him and then had received a long letter from him written in the best of spirits on the twenty-eighth of December. All our friends and acquaintances would have been justified in believing he would outlive me by thirty years. Alas, the physical aches of old age are by no means the most painful. What the loss of Ries means for art all Europe knows. He was one of those few who earn their reputation with profound works which continue to live beyond their time. But reflection on this noble life dedicated to art still engenders within me a strange melancholy feeling — sorrow, actually — since we were bound together for many years by the closest friendship. His devotion to me as an older friend was exceeded perhaps only by his well-founded love for his father. I accompanied him either in person or in spirit from his earliest childhood through the unforgettable years of apprenticeship with Beethoven, the first emergence of his brilliance in Germany, Russia and England, to the many triumphs which England, Germany, and France accorded the mature artist and conductor of great music.

As a person Ries was also a man of remarkable character. He was a noble man in the full sense of the word, a man without falsehood, a man warm and generous. Ries was indeed one of the very rarest of beings, the very pattern of faithfulness and love, as son, brother, husband, father, and friend. I was privileged to know intimately his faultless nature and his genuine, fervent love for the good and beautiful, the muses of his every thought. Recollections of him are among my tenderest, though most melancholy, memories in the evening of my long life. Ries first found himself through his great master and friend Beethoven, and to him he remained faithful in unchanging devotion and gratitude until his final breath. The recording of these notes, especially those dealing with their time spent together, was the most urgent business of the last months, indeed the last weeks and days, of his life. Alas, he had no premonition of how soon he was to follow his cherished master! — And how candidly, yet tenderly, he had depicted Beethoven and his relations with him. — Indeed, he could not have created a more beautiful memorial to his master than these unadorned stories. Moreover, he has woven himself into this picture with such an amiable frankness and modesty that the future biographer of Ries must consult above all Ries's own disclosures about Beethoven if he has any desire to paint a genuine portrait of the most faithful of pupils and masters.

But it is time to put an end to this involuntary outbreak of feeling. Old age is garrulous and it is not easy to fall silent when the subject is so great and the heart is so full.

Wegeler

Coblenz, May 1838

PART ONE

Preface

When an affectionate friendship forms between young people during seven or eight years in their own hometown and develops and deepens as they mature, when as grown men these friends share their lives in a foreign capital for nearly two years and since then, though separated, have remained in close contact for thirty years, then after the death of one — especially one whose outstanding achievement in the field of science or art has secured him lasting European fame — the surviving friend may consider himself justified, even obliged, not to withhold from the world any information which might contribute to a just appreciation of that man and artist.

These few words above characterize my relationship to Ludwig van Beethoven. I was born in Bonn in 1765. In 1782 I became acquainted with the twelve-year-old youth, already a composer, and I remained in constant and closest communication with him until September 1787 when I entered school in Vienna to complete my medical studies.[1] When I returned in October 1789 our same cordial relationship continued until Beethoven later departed for Vienna towards the end of 1792.

I followed in October 1794.* Here we were reunited once more with the same undiminished warmth of feeling and hardly a day passed when we did not meet.

In the middle of the year 1796 I returned to Bonn and we began to exchange letters. During that period of great stress this exchange could hardly be called very active. However, there was little necessity for a lively correspondence on either side since we were kept otherwise informed of each other's changing destinies — he through Simrock's business letters and through my letters to my brother-in-law Stephen von Breuning as well as to friends and colleagues of mine to whom I had introduced Beethoven; and I through the same sources and through letters from Ferdinand Ries.

The following notes will furnish the reader proof that an unbroken exchange of letters was not in the least necessary to sustain our affectionate relations.

I feel it necessary to mention that I have set down in the following pages only what I know for certain. Consequently a

---

* As Rector of the University of Bonn I had signed the decree of the Academic Senate intending to stop the spread of hospital fever by forbidding the students to visit those Frenchmen captured at Quesnoi, Landrecies, Condé, etc., then being transported to Austria. Alms intended for the prisoners were to be brought to them by certain clergymen. The *Moniteur* received this decree some ten or twelve days later and without a hearing branded me a rabid enemy of the Republic. Those were evil times! The people's representative in Bonn gave orders that he was to be addressed with the familiar *du* form. At that time *la queue de Robespierre* was hardly less dangerous than his head had been and it was advisable to save my own.

somewhat exaggerated insistence on providing proof of almost every statement may become apparent. This applies also to the contributions of my friend Ries. However, this also gives us the right to expect that these contributions will correct many a mistake and many unfounded or distorted details in the writings on Beethoven and may thus be considered as genuine source material in this respect.

Since I am no more than a poor dilettante as far as music is concerned, the reader will find among the statements on Beethoven as an artist only those which do not go beyond my sphere. Even when describing how Beethoven accompanied the *Lamentations* I called upon Ries's father for assistance.

Wegeler

Coblenz, May 1838

Ludwig van Beethoven's Family and His Birth

Since so many contradictory reports of Beethoven's origins, family, and date of birth have been circulated, it does not seem out of place to document these notes with accurate, though perhaps too detailed, proof.

The Cologne Electoral Court Calendar for 1760 furnishes on page nine the following information about grandfather Ludwig and father Johann van Beethoven:

Electoral Chamber, Orchestra and Court Music

. . .

Vocalists

Ludwig van Beethoven, Vocalist

. . .

Johann van Beethoven, Unpaid assistant

For the year 1761 the Court Calendar, page nine, contains the entry:

Kapellmeister

Vacant

Vocalists

Herr Ludwig van Beethoven

Johann van Beethoven, Unpaid assistant

In the Court Calendar for the year 1763, page fourteen, the former is entered as Kapellmeister and the latter as full vocalist.

The mother of our Ludwig was Maria Magdalena

Kewerich. The parish records of Ehrenbreitstein give the date of her baptism, which was usually the actual day of birth or certainly the day after.[2]

> Anno 1746, 20$^{ma.}$ Decembris, renata est *Maria Magdalena Kewerich,* Domini *Henrici Kewerich*, coqui primarii Em^{mi} et *Mariae Westorfs*[3], conjugum legitima filia.

From this we can see that she was born in Ehrenbreitstein near Coblenz, the daughter of the chef of the Elector of Trier who had his residence there. Her first marriage had been to the Elector's valet Laym:

> Anno 1763, 30$^{ma.}$ Januarii prævia dispensatione super omnibus denunciationibus de expressa licentia Em$^{mi.}$ sub vesperam in sacello apud R. R. P. P. Capucinos coram requisitis testibus . . . matrimonialiter copulati sunt praenobilis Dominus *Johannes Laym*, Em$^{mi.}$ Cubicularius et praenobilis virgo *Maria Magdalena Kewerich*, Vallensis. (i.e. from the valley).
>
> — Extract from the parish marriage register.

Laym died at the age of thirty, two years and ten months later:

> Anno 1763, 28va Novembris obiit . . . praenobilis Dominus *Johannes Laym*, Em$^{mi.}$ cubicularius etc.
>
> — Extract from the parish register of Ehrenbreitstein

***

This next extract is taken from the parish register of St. Remigius in Bonn.

> 12. November 1767.
>
> Copulavi *Johannem van Beethoven*, filium legitimum *Ludovici van Beethoven* et *Mariae Josephae Poll*,
>
> et
>
> *Mariam Magdalenam Keferich* viduam *Leym* ex

Ehrenbreitstein, filiam *Henrici Keferich* et *Annae Mariae Westorffs.*[4]

(The place in question is sometimes called Thal, sometimes Ehrenbreitstein and sometimes Thal-Ehrenbreitstein.)

The somewhat languid Bonn dialect, which is similar to that spoken in Cologne, turned Kewerich into Keferich and Laym into Leym.

To this marriage was born on 2 April 1769[5] Ludwig Maria whose godparents were grandfather Ludwig van Beethoven and Anna Maria Lohe, called Courtin.[6] This child died on the eighth of that month.

Our Ludwig was born on 17 December 1770[7] as is absolutely clear from the following document:

(Official stamp)

Administrative District of Cologne

District of Bonn. Office of the Lord Mayor of Bonn.

Extract from the parish baptismal register of St. Remigius in Bonn, filed at the office of the Lord Mayor of Bonn.

Anno millesimo septingentesimo septuagesimo, die decima septima Decembris baptizatus est ***Ludovicus***, Domini *Johannis van Beethoven* et *Helenae Keverichs*, conjugum filius legitimus: Patrini: Dominus *Ludovicus van Beethoven*, et *Gertrudis Müllers*, dicta Baums.

This extract certified correct:

Bonn, 28th June 1827.

Lord Mayor

(Seal) (Signed) Windeck.

Since *Lenchen* and *Lene* are diminutives for both *Magdalena* and *Helene*, the mother has obviously been mistakenly entered above as Helene instead of Magdalena.

For these extracts from the official records I am indebted partly to Father Geschwind, Vicar of Ehrenbreitstein, and partly to my childhood friend, Lord Mayor Windeck of Bonn, who spared no effort in seeking out everything that could in any way shed light on Beethoven's family and birth.

***

The nonsense concocted by Fayolle and Choron that Beethoven was the off-spring of Friedrich Wilhelm II, King of Prussia[(1)] needs no refutation. The monarch was not in Bonn prior to Beethoven's birth nor did his mother ever leave the city during her married life.[(2)] This vulgar foolishness is surpassed only by the amusing ignorance of an English author who found the idea that Friedrich II should be Beethoven's father hilarious on the grounds that this king had of course died in 1740.[(3)][9]

But in 1837 even this nonsense was, it seems difficult to believe, considerably outdone by W. van Marsdyk from Holland. This man, in a printed letter addressed *à Monsieur le*

---

(1) *Conversations-Lexicon*, fifth edition, p. 621.

(2) Beethoven expresses himself about this in his letter of 7 December 1826 [*sic*, see p. 40].

(3) "That Beethoven is a wonderful man, there can be no doubt; but if this prince were really his father, he is the greatest prodigy the world ever saw, or most likely will see again: for as Frederick II died in 1740, the period of Mad. Beethoven's gestation must in such a case have been exactly thirty years."

(*The Harmonicon*, November 1823.)

Bourgmestre de la ville de Bonn, claimed our Beethoven was Dutch. The grounds? "If he were really German, he would be called Ludwig von Rübengärten (Ludwig of the beet gardens). Beethoven had in common with Napoleon not only a general uncertainty about his birth date, but also *Lodewyk van Beethoven et Napoleone Buonaparte ont nombre égal de lettres!*"

Furthermore, old inhabitants of Zütphen remembered that Beethoven was born in a hostel built for travelling musicians which has since disappeared (though the site is now no doubt marked by a monument!). — Thus was Beethoven, recognized already as a hero on the very day of his birth, indeed "the greatest prodigy the world ever saw, or most likely will ever see again! — "

Has the reader had enough?

Quand l'absurde est outré, l'on lui fait trop d'honneur
De vouloir par raison combattre son erreur.

As for the house where Beethoven was born, it would seem in all probability to be the Graus house in the Bonngasse, the fourth on the right from the Judengässchen and bearing the number 515, opposite the present Post House. When a child is born, it is the custom for parents who have no relatives in the neighborhood to ask the neighbors to stand as baptismal witnesses. Ludwig Maria's godmother, Frau Courtin, was a neighbor from the house to the right; the godmother of our Ludwig, Frau Baums, was the next-door neighbor to the left (No. 516).

Furthermore Frau Mertens, née Lengersdorf, whose parental home was diagonally opposite the house where

Beethoven was born, remembers quite clearly that Beethoven was in fact born in this particular house.

Beethoven's birthplace

⁂

Two more sons were born after our Beethoven, the elder Caspar Anton Carl on 8 April 1774, the younger Nicolaus Johannes on 2 October 1776. — Caspar's godparents were the Minister Plenipotentiary von Belderbusch and the Abbess of Vylich, Countess von Satzenhofen. Caspar later earned his living as a piano teacher. Nicolaus studied pharmacy in the Court Pharmacy in Bonn. Both of them followed Ludwig to Vienna where they lived under the names of Carl and Johann.

Ludwig's grandfather died on 24 December 1773; his mother, 17 July 1787; his father, 18 December 1792; his brother Caspar or Carl in the last quarter of 1815. Johann is probably still alive and living in Vienna.

Beethoven's Education and First Schooling

Ludwig van Beethoven received as a young boy his first instruction in music from his father who was, as mentioned earlier, a tenor in the service of the Elector Max Friedrich residing in Bonn. The father was, however, not a pianist. His grandfather, the kapellmeister and bass singer, had once produced operas at the National Theater built by the Elector. Among the other singers at that theater were two sisters of the famous Salomon, who was born in Bonn in 1745 and died in London in 1815; the kapellmeister's son, father of our Beethoven; and a married woman named Drever, who was the sister of the old but still vigorous father Franz Ries, the elder. The grandfather was said to have been much applauded, especially in the operetta *L'Amore Artigiano (Love Among the Artisans)*[10] and in the *Deserteur von Monsigny*.

Little Louis clung with great affection to this grandfather, who as noted above, was also Beethoven's godfather, and even though he lost him so soon, he retained the most vivid, early impression of him. He was fond of talking about his grandfather with his childhood friends, and his pious and gentle mother, whom he loved much more than his very strict father, was often obliged to tell him about his grandfather. The portrait of him by the court painter Radoux was the only thing which he had sent to Vienna from Bonn and it gave him much pleasure his entire life. This grandfather was a short, sturdy man with extremely animated eyes and was highly respected as an artist.

Our Beethoven was also, as Ritter von Seyfried correctly describes him, "of sturdy build, medium height, strong-boned, full of vitality, a picture of strength."

Beethoven's education was neither particularly neglected nor especially good. He learned his reading, writing, arithmetic, and a little Latin in a public school where the present President of the County Court at Coblenz, Herr Wurzer, was a fellow pupil. Music he learned at home and he was constantly and strictly kept at it by his father. The family enjoyed no income other than the father's salary and consequently their circumstances were somewhat straitened. The father, not particularly distinguished for either his intellect or his morals, was rather strict since he hoped to find in his eldest son a help in the upbringing of the other children.

Ludwig made his first acquaintance with German literature, especially poetry, in the von Breuning family in Bonn where he also received his first introduction to social life and behavior. As this family will be mentioned repeatedly in the future, this would seem to be the proper place to describe its members and Beethoven's relations with them.

The family consisted of the mother, who was the widow of the Court Councilor von Breuning, three sons of about Beethoven's age, and one daughter. Beethoven taught the daughter as well as the youngest son, who had become an excellent pianist by the time he died in 1798 just after finishing his medical studies. The second son, Stephen von Breuning, became an Imperial Court Councilor in Vienna. He remained a loyal friend throughout Beethoven's entire life and died very soon after him. The third, Christoph von Breuning, is *Geheimer-Revisions-und Cassations-Rath* in Berlin. The daughter, Eleonora von Breuning, to whom he dedicated the *Variations No. 1*, is the wife of the author of these pages.

The von Breuning family, silhouette, 1782

An unforced atmosphere of culture reigned in the house in spite of an abundance of youthful high spirits. Christoph von Breuning experimented with little verses at an early age as did Stephen von Breuning much later, not without success. Friends of the house excelled in the sort of sociable entertainment that unites usefulness with pleasure.

If we also add that the family enjoyed a good measure of affluence, especially before the war, it is easy to understand that Beethoven's youthful exuberance first developed there.

Beethoven was soon treated as one of the children in the family and not only did he spend the greatest part of the day there but even many nights. He felt free there, he could move around with ease, and everything combined to make him cheerful and to develop his mind. Being five years older than Beethoven, I was able to observe and form a judgment on these things. The mother of the von Breuning family, who was

The von Breuning family house

born on 3 January 1750 and is living with me still, had great power over the boy, who was frequently stubborn and unsociable. Everything here can be confirmed by numerous passages in Beethoven's letters.

⁂

However, let us return to Beethoven's musical education.

Again, he received his first instruction from his father.

Later on he had much better schooling from a certain Pfeiffer, a music director and oboist subsequently engaged as a conductor in Düsseldorf for the band of the Bavarian Regiment. Pfeiffer was known as an excellent artist and extremely bright man. Beethoven owed the most to this teacher and was so grateful that through Simrock he provided him with financial support even from Vienna.

Whether he received instruction from the court organist van der Eder[11] after Pfeiffer's departure from Bonn, I do not know, but I think it most likely because I do not know of anyone else from whom he might have learned the technique of organ playing. When the famous organist Abbé Vogler played in Bonn, I was sitting at Beethoven's sickbed.

Neefe, the former musical director of the Grossmann Theater Company later employed as court organist and known as a composer, had little influence on the instruction of our Ludwig; indeed he complained about Neefe's excessively harsh criticism of his first attempts at composition.[12]

In 1785 Beethoven was engaged as organist of the Electoral Chapel by Elector Max Franz, the brother of Emperor Joseph II, where he alternated with Neefe in duties hardly strenuous. In making this appointment the Elector apparently was thinking only of Beethoven's need for support.

Ritter von Seyfried is mistaken when he states in his *Ludwig van Beethoven's Studies*, page four: "Now that young Beethoven was no less competent on the organ, the art-loving

Elector nominated him as Neefe's successor."[12a] Neefe and Beethoven were court organists at the same time.

Christian Gottlob Neefe (1748-1798)

In the Cologne Court for the year 1790, page sixteen, is the entry:

Electoral chamber, chapel and court music
Organists
Christian Neefe
Ludwig van Beethoven

The duties of an organist at court were slight. Furthermore the organ was small, in keeping with the size of the court chapel (the present Protestant church), and was not even visible to the congregation. Great skill in playing was not required; indeed it could hardly even be put to use consider-

---

(1) Neefe was a fine example of the attitude prevalent at the time, since he was the organist of a prince of the church although he was a Protestant himself.

ing the limitations of the instrument. Neefe was also in good health and not prevented from executing his duties by other business[1]. Thus, as already suggested, Beethoven's appointment was obviously intended only as a most tactfully extended support.

But who helped him to obtain this post? A man who, as far I know, has never been given the credit he deserves in writings about Beethoven.

Count Ferdinand von Waldstein (1762-1823)

Beethoven's first and in every respect most important patron, his Mæcenas, was Count Waldstein, Knight of the Teutonic Order and, what is most important in this connection, favorite and constant companion of the young Elector. Subsequently he became Commander of the Teutonic Order at Virnsberg and Exchequer to the Emperor of Austria. Not just a connoisseur, he was also a practicing musician. It was he who in every way possible supported our Beethoven and first appreciated his genius to the full. With his assistance the young artist developed the talent for extemporizing and improvising variations on a given theme. From him he often received financial support, bestowed with such consideration for his easily wounded feelings that Beethoven usually assumed they were small gratuities from the Elector. Beethoven's appointment as organist, his being sent by the Elector to Vienna, etc., were all the Count's doing. That Beethoven dedicated the great and important *Sonata in C Major, Opus 53,* to him in later years is proof of the undiminished gratitude of the mature man.

Count Waldstein was the man Beethoven had to thank that the first blossoming of his genius was not suppressed, and so we, too, are indebted to this Mæcenas for Beethoven's later glory.

But let us return to our organist.

In his new position Beethoven first casually proved his talent to the orchestra by the following incident: In the Catholic church the Lamentations of Jeremiah are sung on three days of Holy Week. These consist of short movements of four to six lines apiece performed as chorales, each to a particular rhythm. The vocal line consisted of four consecutive notes, for example *c, d, e, f,* with several words or even complete sentences changed on the third until a few notes at the end lead back to the key-note. Since the organ must remain silent during these three days, the singer receives only an improvised accompaniment from a pianist.

Once when it was Beethoven's turn to perform this duty, he asked the singer Heller, who was very secure indeed in his intonation, whether he might try to throw him off, and he used the rather rashly given permission to wander about so much in the accompaniment that the singer was completely bewildered and could no longer find the closing cadence, even though Beethoven kept striking the note to be chanted in the treble with his little finger.

Franz Anton Ries, then first violinist and musical director of the Electoral Chapel, is still fond of relating in detail how Kapellmeister Luchesi, who was present, was startled by Beethoven's playing. In his first flush of anger Heller complained to the Elector about Beethoven and although the clever young Elector, who could be quite mischievous himself at times, was amused by the whole story, he nevertheless commanded that a simpler accompaniment be played in future.

At that time Beethoven also became a Chamber Musician. Once he played in that capacity before the Elector in a small group with the elder Ries and the famous Bernhard Romberg[13] who is still alive today. The artists were sightreading a new trio by Pleyel. In the second part of the Adagio, they were not able to stay together although they did not break down completely. They kept on playing courageously and luckily reached the end at the same time. Afterwards they figured out that two bars had been left out of the piano part. The Elector was very intrigued by Pleyel's composition and had it repeated a week later when their secret was discovered, much to the Prince's delight.

⁂

When Haydn first returned from England, a breakfast was given for him by the Electoral Orchestra in Godesberg, a resort near Bonn. On this occasion Beethoven showed him a cantata. Haydn examined it very closely and then warmly encouraged the composer to pursue his studies. Later this cantata was supposed to be performed in Mergentheim, but several sections were so difficult for the wind instruments that some musicians declared they could not possibly play them. As a result, the performance was cancelled. As far as we know, this cantata was never printed.[14]

***

Beethoven's first compositions were the sonatas published in Speyer's *Blumenlese,* followed by the song *Wenn jemand eine Reise thut,* then the music to a *Ritter-ballet* performed by the high nobility during Carnival season but not yet published.[15] The piano score is at present in the hands of the music publisher Dunst in Frankfurt who will presumably include it in the edition of Beethoven's works he is now completing. This edition of the *Ritter-ballet* should also include a minstrel's song, a German song, a drinking song, etc. Since Beethoven had not indicated himself as composer of these songs, the compositions were long assumed to be the work of Count Waldstein, especially since the Count had put the ballet together in collaboration with the dancing master Habich from Aachen.

Next came the Variations on *Vieni amore,* a theme by Righini, dedicated to the Countess of Hatzfeld. These Variations gave rise to the following unusual incident. Because he had not yet heard any great or celebrated pianists, Beethoven knew nothing of the finer nuances of handling the instrument; his playing was rough and hard. While on a journey from Bonn to Mergentheim, where the Elector kept a residence as Grand Master of the Teutonic Order, Beethoven and the Elector's Orchestra stopped in Aschaffenburg. Ries, Simrock, and the two Rombergs took him to Sterkel who, in response to everyone's request, sat himself down to play. Sterkel's playing was very light, highly pleasing, and, as the elder Ries put it, somewhat ladylike. Beethoven stood beside him concentrating intensely. Then he was asked to play but only complied when Sterkel intimated that he doubted whether even the composer of the Variations could play them all the way through. Beethoven played not only these variations, as far as he could remember them (Sterkel could not find the music), but also a number of others no less difficult and, to the amazement of his listeners, he played everything in precisely the same pleasant manner with which Sterkel had impressed him. That is how easy it was for him to adapt his style of playing to someone else's.[16]

⁂

This journey, incidentally, on which the whole orchestra travelled in two yachts up the Rhine and the Main during the most beautiful season of the year, was an abundant source of the loveliest memories for Beethoven. Lux, the singer and famous comedian, was elected Great King of the

Journey. Parcelling out duties, he assigned Beethoven and Bernhard Romberg to the kitchen and, indeed, they did serve there. Beethoven's diploma promoting him through the kitchen ranks, awarded on the Heights of Rüdesheim, will probably have been found among his effects. I certainly saw it in his possession, lovingly kept, in 1796. A large seal in pitch affixed to the lid of a box and attached with a few unravelled strands of the ship's rigging gave this diploma a most ceremonious aspect.

From his earliest youth Beethoven had an extraordinary aversion to teaching. At times Frau von Breuning would try to force him to continue teaching in the house of the Austrian Ambassador, the Duke of Westphalia, which was opposite her own[(1)]. He would set out, *ut iniquae mentis asellus*[(2)/**16a**], because he knew he was being observed. However, he often turned around at the very door of the house, ran back, and promised he would teach for two hours the next day, it was simply not possible for him that day. His own personal hardships were not enough to persuade him to teach, only perhaps the thought of his family and in particular of his dear mother.

Later on, after Beethoven had become prominent in Vienna, he developed a similar, if not even stronger, aversion to being asked to play at social occasions, and each time he was asked his good humor disappeared entirely. Many times

---

(1) Now the Furstenberg residence
(2) Like a bad-tempered little donkey—Horace

he came to me, gloomy and upset, complaining that he was forced to play even if the blood burned under his nails. I would try to amuse him and calm him down until gradually a conversation would develop between us. When I had managed this, I would let the conversation drop and seat myself at the writing table. If Beethoven wished to continue talking with me, he had to sit on the chair in front of the piano. Soon he would aimlessly strike a few chords, often still turned away from the instrument, and from these he would gradually develop the most beautiful melodies. Oh, how I wished I understood more about music! Several times I casually placed music paper on a nearby stand, hoping to obtain a manuscript from him; he would cover it with writing, but then he would fold it up and put it in his pocket! All I could do was laugh at myself. — About his playing I was allowed to say nothing, or at best make only a passing remark. He would then leave in a completely different mood and was always glad to come back. His aversion to playing in company, however, remained and was frequently a source of considerable dissension between Beethoven and the best of his friends and patrons.

⁂

One day Beethoven was improvising at the von Breuning house (where he was frequently asked to describe in music the character of some mutual acquaintance) and the elder Ries was urged to accompany him on the violin. After some hesitation he consented and that may well have been the first time the two artists had improvised together — a beautiful, very charming manner of playing. Later Ries and his son Ferdinand sometimes treated their audiences at public concerts to this unexpected pleasure.

⁂

Rather than continue to observe a more or less chronological order as I have done so far, I would like to offer the rest of my remarks on Beethoven as notes to the letters which follow. This method offers a very convenient way for me to recall interesting details and I imagine the reader will also welcome this change. Some of Beethoven's letters to me, therefore, are reprinted below. The first has already been published in the *Allgemeine Theater-Zeitung* in Vienna (No. 37, 25 March 1828). It is, as I remarked then, probably the longest my immortal friend ever wrote. On its first publication I commented: "This serves to prove a great deal of what I have said about Beethoven's education in the von Breuning household. Also in this letter, certainly for the first time, he pours out his heart concerning his deafness, and confides many details of his plans, etc. Taken as a whole, it is a pure expression of his heart, and the reader will know our friend much more closely when he has examined this letter." From now on Beethoven is no longer a stranger. A relationship has been established, based on deeper knowledge of the man and the artist, the foundation of sincere and lasting respect.

The letter was copied from the *Theater-Zeitung* by the *Bonner Wochenblatt* (No. 25, 1829) and finally, to the best of my knowledge, by the *Conversations-Blatt* in the *Ober-Post-*

Amts-Zeitung a few days after it had been read in the Frankfurt museum (at the beginning of 1836). A French translation appeared in the *Journal des débats* on 20 March 1838.

None of the other letters has ever been printed or reproduced before.[17]

⁂

Vienna, June 29, 1800[(1)]

My dear, kind Wegeler,

How grateful I am for your remembering me; I have so little deserved it or sought to deserve it from you. Yet you are so very good; you are not deterred by anything, not even my unpardonable negligence. You always remain the loyal, good, honest friend. — You must not believe, no, never, that I could forget you and all the others who were so kind and dear to me. There are moments when I long for your company; indeed I yearn to spend some time there with you. — My fatherland, the lovely countryside where I first saw the light of day, seems in my mind's eye still as beautiful and vivid as when I left you. I know that rejoining you and greeting our Father Rhine once more will be one of the happiest moments in my life. — When that may be I cannot yet say. — But I do want to assure you that when we meet again you will find me a much greater person, not only as an artist but also as a man, better and more fully developed. And if our Fatherland is more prosperous then, my art shall prove itself only for the benefit of the poor.[(2)] *O blessed moment, how happy I am that I can summon you, that I can create you myself! — You want to know something about my situation; well, at present it is not so bad. Unbelievable though it may seem when I tell you, Lichnowsky*[(3)] *has always been and remains my warmest friend (of course there have been slight misunderstandings between us, but haven't they only strengthened our friendship? —).*[(4)] *Last year he set aside a fixed sum of 600 florins on which I can draw until I find a position suitable for me. My compositions bring in a considerable amount, and I might say that I have more commissions than I can possibly honor. I can also count on six or seven publishers for each thing, and even more, should I want them. People no longer bargain with me; I demand and they pay. You can see that this is a rather nice situation. For instance, when I see a friend in need and my own purse at the moment does not allow me to help him immediately, I have only to set myself down and within a short time I can come to his aid. — I also live more economically than I used to; if I remain here for good I should certainly be able to secure one day for an Academy concert every year. I have already given several.*[(5)] *Only the evil demon, my miserable health, has done me an evil turn: my hearing has become steadily weaker these last three years. This disability is supposed to have been originally caused by the condition of my stomach, which, as you know, has always been wretched*[(6)] *but has become worse here. I suffer constantly from diarrhea and consequently am extraordinarily debilitated. Frank wanted to restore the* **tone** *of my body with strengthening medicines*[(7)] *and my hearing with almond oil, but — wouldn't you know it! — nothing changed. My hearing grew steadily worse and my stomach remained in the same state as before; this continued until the autumn of last year, and I was sometimes really in despair. Then a medical* **asinus** *advised cold baths for my condition. A more intelligent doctor ordered the customary lukewarm bath in the Danube. That worked miracles — my stomach improved, although my hearing problem remained, or worsened. This last winter I was truly miserable. I had really dreadful attacks of colic and deteriorated again to my previous state. And thus it remained until about four weeks ago, when I went to Vering*[(8)]*, thinking that my condition might also require the attention of a surgeon. Besides I have always had confidence in him. He managed to stop the violent diarrhea almost* *always had confidence in him. He managed to stop the violent diarrhea almost entirely. He prescribed baths in lukewarm water from the Danube, into which I had to pour a flask of strengthening stuff each time, and gave me no medicine at all until about four days ago when he ordered pills for the stomach and an infusion for the ear. As a result I can only say I feel stronger and better, save my ears which buzz and ring day and night. I spend my life miserably, I must confess; for almost two years I have avoided all society, because I cannot say to people: I am deaf. If I had any other profession, it would not be quite so bad, but in my profession this is a dreadful position. And then there are my enemies, whose number is not small; what would they not say! — I can give you some idea of this peculiar deafness, when I must tell you that in the theater I have to get very close to the orchestra to understand the performers, and that from a distance I do not hear the high notes of the instruments and the singers' voices. It is surprising that there are people who have never noticed this when speaking to me*(9)*. Since I have usually been absent-minded, they take it for that. Sometimes too I hardly hear people who speak softly. The sound I can hear, it is true, but not the words. And yet if anyone shouts, I can't bear it. What will become of me Heaven alone knows. Vering tells me that my hearing will certainly get better, even if I don't recover completely. I have so often cursed . . . my existence. Plutarch has taught me resignation. I will, if at all possible, defy my fate, although there will be moments in my life when I shall be the unhappiest of God's creatures. I beg you to say nothing about my condition to anyone, not even to Lorchen*(10)*. I am confiding this to you only as a secret, but I would be grateful if sometime you would correspond with Vering about it. If my condition continues like this, I will visit you next spring. You will rent a house for me in some beautiful part of the country, and for half a year I will lead the life of a peasant. Perhaps that will change things. Resignation! What a miserable refuge, and yet for me it is all that remains.*

You will forgive me, I'm sure, for burdening you with a friend's troubles, even though you yourself already have troubles enough. Steffen Breuning is now here and we are together almost daily. It does me so much good to revive the old feelings of friendship again. He really has become a fine, splendid young man who knows a thing or two and — like all of us, more or less — has his heart in the right place. I now have very nice rooms overlooking the Bastei(11) *which is extremely beneficial to my health. I do believe I will be*

Stephan von Breuning (1774-1827)

able to arrange for Breuning to join me. — I shall send you your Antiochum(12)*, and also a great deal of my music, if you do not think that it will cost you too much. Honestly, your love for art still gives me great pleasure. Just write to me how it may be done and I will send you all my compositions, a fair number by now, of course, and daily increasing. — In return for the portrait of my grandfather which I beg you to send me by mail coach as soon as possible, I am sending you one of his grandson, your ever fond and loving Beethoven. This portrait is being published here by Artaria, who often asked me for it, as did many others, including foreign art dealers. — I shall write to Stoffel*(13) *soon and give him a piece of my mind about his stubbornness. I will shout at* *him about our old friendship until his ears ring, and he will have to promise me faithfully not to hurt you anymore, especially as your present circumstances are troubled enough. — I shall also write to dear Lorchen. Never have I forgotten any of you dear, kind people, even though I have not written you at all. But writing, as you know, was never my strong point. Even my best friends have not received any letters from me for years. I live only in my music, and one composition is hardly finished before another is already begun. The way I write now, I often do three or four things at once. — Do write me more often now; I shall make an effort to find time to write you occasionally. Give my regards to everyone, and to our kind Frau Hofräthin*(14) *and tell her that I still have a "raptus" now and again*(15). *As regards the Koches I am not at all surprised about the change in circumstances. Fortune is round as a ball and naturally does not always come to rest with the noblest and the best. — Concerning Ries, to whom I send my warmest greetings, I will write to you in more detail about his son, although I think that he would probably have better luck in Paris than in Vienna; Vienna is deluged with people and even the best talents are sometimes hard put to make a living. — In the autumn or winter I shall see what I can do for him, because then everyone rushes back to town. Farewell, my good, faithful Wegeler. Rest assured of the love and friendship of your*

Beethoven

Explanation of the notes to the above letter.

(1) The year is missing; from the subsequent letter, however, it becomes clear that it was in all probability 1800.[18]

(2) Because of the war, Bonn had lost its Elector, court, government offices, university, army, in short all its sources of income. It had never had any factories or commercial traffic.

(3) Carl, Prince Lichnowsky, Count Werdenberg, Dynast of Granson, was a great benefactor, indeed friend, of Beethoven. The Prince even took Beethoven into his house as a guest, where he remained for at least a few years. I found him there toward the end of 1794 and he was still there when I left in the middle of 1796. However, Beethoven almost always kept lodgings in the country at the same time.

The Prince was a great lover and connoisseur of music. He played the piano, and by studying Beethoven's works and playing them more or less well, he tried to prove to Beethoven that he did not need to change anything in his style of composition, even though the difficulties of his works were often pointed out to him. There were performances at the Prince's house every Friday morning. Besides our friend, four salaried musicians — Schuppanzigh, Weiss, Kraft,[19] and one other (Link?) — and usually also an amateur, Zmeskall, took part. Beethoven always accepted the comments of these gentlemen with pleasure. Once when I was there, for instance, Kraft, the famous cellist, pointed out to him that he should mark a passage in the finale of the third trio, *Opus 1*, with *sulla corda G* and that in the second of these trios the finale, which Beethoven had marked 4/4, should be changed to 2/4.

Beethoven's new compositions were first performed here whenever they were suitable. Several great musicians and music lovers usually gathered to hear them. When I lived in Vienna I was usually, though not always, present. It was there that Beethoven first played for old Haydn the three sonatas which he dedicated to him. Here, in 1795, Count

Appony commissioned Beethoven to compose for a fixed fee a quartet, a form in which he had produced nothing so far. The Count announced that he did not wish to reserve the quartet for himself for six months before publication as was customary, nor did he demand a dedication, etc.

I repeatedly reminded Beethoven of this commission and he settled down to work on it twice. However, the first attempt turned into a grand string trio *(Opus 3)*, the second into a string quintet *(Opus 4)*.[1]

It was also here that another Hungarian count (at my encouragement when he told me what he wished to do) once laid before Beethoven a manuscript copy of a difficult Bach composition. Beethoven played the piece at sight and,

---

(1)— Whether and to what extent the following remarks about the composition of quartets apply to Beethoven, I gladly leave to the judgment of the masters in this art. They naturally reminded me of the facts mentioned here.

"The string quartet is the most difficult and in a way also the most thankless form of musical composition both for the composer and for the performer. No work requires such profound, thorough knowledge of freeflowing yet controlled composition, so much delicacy, tenderness, and refinement of taste, and so much depth and profundity of the spirit as does the string quartet. It is, so to speak, the ultimate in all instrumental music. Here, in a small framework and with but four instruments, all the life and depth of music must be delineated in its most delicate outline. For this the orchestra commands a hundred instruments as well as an overall canvas where, because of its very scale, painstaking individual and delicate attention to detail becomes a mistake."

— *Frankfurter Conversations-Blatt* No. 353 — 21 December 1836

according to the owner, just as Bach himself had played it. A Viennese composer, Förster, once brought him a quartet which he had copied out only that very morning. When in the second part of the first movement the cello lost his place, Beethoven stood up and sang the bass accompaniment while continuing to play his own part. When I pointed this out as a mark of extraordinary skill, he answered with a smile: "The bass line had to run that way, unless the author knew nothing about composition." — In response to another remark that he had played a presto passage which he had never seen before so fast that it must have been virtually impossible to have seen the individual notes, he replied, "That is not in the least bit necessary. When you are reading rapidly there may be any number of printing errors which you do not see or pay any attention to, provided the language is familiar to you."

The musicians usually stayed for dinner after the concert. Artists and scholars also gathered here with no distinction made as to social standing. Princess Christiane was the highly educated daughter of Count Franz Joseph von Thun, incidentally a most charitable and honourable gentleman himself though prone to excess romanticism because of his association with Lavater. It was well known that he believed he could heal sickness through the power of his right hand (See *Conversations-Lexicon*, Seventh edition, vol. 11, p. 236).

(4) Beethoven was highly sensitive and consequently easily provoked. However, if one waited for the air to clear after the first explosion, he could listen to remonstrances with a willing ear and a conciliatory heart. As a result he always apologized

for much more than he was guilty of. For instance I possess a little note from him which I received in Vienna where he says, among other things, "What a detestable picture you have shown me of myself! Oh, I realize I do not deserve your friendship, . . . It was not intentional, premeditated malice on my part that made me treat you that way; it was my unpardonable thoughtlessness." . . . He goes on in this manner for three pages and then ends with: "But — no more. I come to you and throw myself into your arms, asking for my lost friend back. Return yourself to me again, to your remorseful, loving friend who will never forget you,

Beethoven[20]

The two letters to Fraulein von Breuning which follow prove the same point.

Subsequently he also broke off his friendship with Stephen von Breuning for some time (— with what friend did he not behave so?).[21] When at last he was convinced by someone else that he had done von Breuning a great injustice, he wrote him in the same contrite fashion. A most sincere reconciliation took place between two and the closest friendship continued uninterrupted until Beethoven's death.

(5) Much has been written about Beethoven's prosperity and poverty. This much I know from personal experience: Beethoven had been brought up in very straitened circumstances and had always been placed under some guardianship, as it were, even if it was only that of his friends. He did not know the value of money and was somewhat less than economical. For instance lunch at the Prince's house was set for

four o'clock. "Consequently," Beethoven said, "I would have to be home by half past three every day, change into something better, see that I was properly shaven, etc. — I can't stand all that!" And so it happened that he frequently went out to eat in taverns. This made matters even worse for him economically because as I've said he understood neither the value of money nor what things should cost.

The Prince, who had a very loud metallic voice, one day instructed his footman that if both he and Beethoven should ring at the same time, Beethoven should be served first. When Beethoven overheard this, he hired a servant of his own that very same day. Similarly, when on a whim he decided that he would like to learn to ride, he hired a horse of his own, even though he had the Prince's entire stable at his disposal.

The financial arrangements for his own works (or as Beethoven aptly put it in a letter to Ferdinand Ries: The honorarium *avec ou sans honneur*) were much more frequently negotiated by his brother Caspar[22] than by himself.

That Beethoven had very little understanding of money matters even as late as 1821 is apparent in one of his letters. I am indebted to the kindness of Polizeirath Guisez in Aachen for providing me with a copy of the original of this letter which is in his possession.

Baden, 27 September 1821

Dear Sir,

Pardon my liberty in troubling you. I have entrusted the bearer of this letter, Herr von —, with a banknote for exchange or sale. Being unfamiliar with everything necessary to such a transaction, I would ask you very kindly to give him your advice and counsel. Several illnesses last winter and summer have set me back somewhat in my financial affairs. I have been here since 7 September and must remain here until the end of October. All this costs a great deal of money and prevents me from earning it in my usual manner. I expect money from abroad, but since the exchange rate is so high at the moment, I feel this is the easiest way to get by for the time being. Later on I shall purchase a new banknote again . . .

Your friend,

Beethoven

(In great haste)

This unsealed letter was in an envelope on which the following was written as a kind of postscript by Beethoven:

You will easily see what kind of business genius I am. Only after the enclosed letter had been written did I discuss the banknote with a friend. It then became clear to me that one need only detach a coupon and the whole matter is taken care of. I am glad therefore that I need not trouble you with it . . . . . .

Yours,

Beethoven.

One might ask: why bother the gentleman with the letter at all, since he apparently did not know him well? The brief request to look after the bearer of the letter, which has been deleted here, would not have required as many lines as did the postscript.

Incidentally, I fully support von Seyfried's opinion on page 27: "Beethoven knew neither ambition (?)[23] nor extravagance, nor did he know the true value of money which he considered merely a means to acquire the absolute bare necessities. Only in his last years did the traces of anxious frugality appear, a trait which did not affect his innate charitable impulses."

Other evidence of his completely disordered financial habits is cited by our friend Ries.

(6) Only on the afternoon two days before the performance of his first concerto (C major) did he write the Rondo. He was suffering at the time from the rather severe colic which plagued him frequently. I helped him with minor remedies as best I could. Four copyists sat in the hallway working from the manuscript sheets he handed over to them one at a time.[24]

Here I may be permitted another digression. During the first rehearsal which took place in Beethoven's room the next day, the piano was a semitone flatter than the wind instruments. Beethoven immediately ordered the winds as well as the other instruments to tune to B flat rather than A and he played his part in C sharp.

(7) Peter Frank, director of medical studies in Pavia, later director of the General Hospital in Vienna, the first classical writer on the enforcement of health laws, etc.[25]

Beethoven probably underlined the word ***tone*** because he could not harmonize it with the beautiful meaning he knew — or was he laughing about it?

(8) Chief medical staff officer, Imperial Councilor, born in Hungary, father of the general practitioner Joseph von Vering, who was famous in France and Germany. This and the following letter show that Beethoven suffered from various other maladies apart from his deafness and that von Seyfried's

statement (p. 13) — "He (Beethoven) knew nothing of illnesses despite his peculiar way of life." — must be taken with great reservation.[26]

(9) Even Ries did not notice it during the first two years, as we will see.

(10) Eleonore von Breuning, Wegeler's wife.

(11) In Pasquillati's house?[27]

(12) A well-known picture by Füger, Director of the Academy of Painting in Vienna, showing Erasistratus perceiving the love of Antiochus for his stepmother Stratonice.

(13) Christoph von Breuning, *Geheimer Revisionsrath* in Berlin.

(14) The mother of the von Breuning family.

(15) When Beethoven, as recounted earlier, suddenly rushed back to the mother of the Breuning family as she stood watching him rather than going to give his lessons, or when he had another of his strokes of genius, as his whims were called, the kind mother used to say with a shrug: "He has his *raptus* again today." A passage in Goethe's *Correspondence with a Child, Part 2*, p. 200, proves that the word and its meaning remained dear to him. Bettina reports: "Last night I wrote down everything. This morning I read it to him (Beethoven)" and he said, "Did I really say that? — Well, then I had a *raptus* again."

⁂

Vienna, 16 November 1801

My dear Wegeler! I thank you for the renewed proof of your solicitude on my behalf, all the more since I deserve it so little. — You want to know how I am, what I need. Much as I dislike discussing such matters at all, I would prefer talking about it with you rather than with anyone else.

For several months now Vering has put plasters on both arms. These consist, as you know, of a certain kind of bark.[1] *This is a most disagreeable procedure, since I am always robbed of the free use of my arms for a few days (until the bark has had sufficient effect), not to mention the pain. True, I cannot deny that the buzzing and ringing in my ears is somewhat less than it was, particularly in my left ear where my hearing problems actually started. But my hearing has certainly not improved; indeed I must admit that I think it is perhaps even worse than before. — My stomach is better. Especially when I take the lukewarm baths for several days running, I am reasonably well for eight or even ten days. I very occasionally take something strengthening for my stomach; I am now starting to use the herbs you prescribed for my stomach. — Vering will hear nothing about shower baths. In general I am thoroughly dissatisfied with him; he shows too little care and understanding of my illness. If I did not go to see him myself, which costs me a great deal of effort, I would never see him at all. — What do you think of Schmidt?*[2] *I do not like changing, but it seems to me that Vering is too much of a practitioner to acquire many new ideas through reading. — Schmidt seems to be quite a different sort of man in this respect and might possibly not be quite so negligent. — One hears marvelous things about galvanism; what do you think of it? One doctor told me he had seen a deaf and dumb child recover his hearing (in Berlin) and a man who was deaf for seven years also regained his hearing. — I have just heard that your Schmidt*[3] *is experimenting with it.*

I live now somewhat more pleasantly again, getting out among people more. You can hardly believe how desolate, how sad my life has been these last two years. My weak hearing haunted me everywhere like a spectre and I fled from people, making myself appear a misanthrope, though I am far from that.

— This change was wrought by a dear, enchanting girl who loves me and whom I love. After two years there are now some blissful moments again; this is the first time that I feel marriage might bring one happiness. Unfortunately she is not of my class(4) *— and now — I could not, of course, marry. — I must struggle on bravely. If it were not for my hearing, I would have long ago traveled round half the world; I still must do it. — For me there is no greater joy than to practice and present my art. — Do not believe that I would be happy with you. And yet what should make me happier? Your very solicitude would hurt me; every moment I would read pity in your faces and that would make me even more miserable. — That lovely native countryside, what was my lot there? Nothing but the hope for a better life. That would be mine now, but for this affliction! Oh, I would embrace the entire world if I were free from this miserable disease. Yes, I really do feel as if my youth were just beginning; was I not always a sickly person? More than ever before my physical strength has been increasing for some time now, my mental powers as well. Each day I get closer to the goal which I can feel but cannot describe. Only in this way can your Beethoven thrive. — Do not speak of rest! — I know of no rest but sleep and it pains me enough that I must now devote more time to sleep than usual. Were I but half delivered from my affliction, then — I would come to you and, as a completely mature man, renew the old feelings of friendship. You shall see me happy again, as happy as it is my lot to be in this world below; not unhappy. — No, I could not bear that. I shall take Fate by the throat; it shall not subdue me entirely. — Oh, it is so beautiful to live life a thousand times! A quiet life — No, I feel I am no longer meant for that — Do please write me as soon as possible. — Make sure that Steffen decides to take a position somewhere in the Teutonic Order.*(5) *Life here is too strenuous for his health. Besides, he leads such an isolated existence that I cannot see at all how he means to get any further. You know what it is like here; I do not mean to say*

that a social life might lessen the strain on him, but one cannot even persuade him to go anywhere. — Some time ago I held a musicale in my home, but our friend Steffen stayed away.(6) *Advise him to rest more and to quiet down; I have tried everything I could; without rest and patience he can never again be happy or healthy*(7). *Tell me in your next letter whether or not it matters if I send you a great deal of music. You can of course sell what you do not need and thereby retrieve your postal expenses. — My portrait, too. Fondest and kindest regards to Lorchen — also to Mama — also to Christoph. You do love me a little, don't you? Be assured of this (my love) as well as the friendship of*

Your Beethoven

Notes

(1) The bark of *Daphne mezereum*

(2) Joh. Adam Schmidt, Councilor, staff surgeon, professor of medicine at the Josephinum, eye specialist, author of several classic writings.

(3) Your Schmidt. I lived in the closest, friendliest contact with Schmidt and Hunczovsky until their deaths. The former wrote under his portrait which he sent to me: *Cogitare ut esse tui, idem est. Wegelero suo Schmidt.*[28]

(4) In the biographical notes which Ignaz von Seyfried appended to his *Studies of Beethoven* the following passage occurs on page 13: "Beethoven was never married and strangely enough never involved in a love affair."[28a] The truth, as my brother-in-law Stephan von Breuning, and Ferdinand Ries, and Bernhard Romberg, and I learned to know it, was that Beethoven was never not in love and was usually involved to a high degree. His and Stephan von Breuning's first love was Miss Jeanette d'Honrath from Cologne, Neumarkt

No. 19 (now the house of Mr. Biercher, the master builder) who often spent a few weeks with the von Breuning family in Bonn. She was a beautiful, vivacious blonde, with a good education and an amiable disposition; she enjoyed music enormously and had a pleasant voice. She often teased our friend by singing a song popular at that time:

> Parting from you this very day,
> And unable to prevent it,
> Is much too painful for my heart!

The favored rival was the Austrian recruiting officer in Cologne, Carl Greth, who married Miss d'Honrath and died as Field Marshal General, Commanding Officer of the 23rd Infantry Regiment, Commander of Temeswar, etc., on 15 October 1827.

Then followed the tenderest affection for the beautiful and cultured Fraulein v. W.[29] Bernhard Romberg told me anecdotes about this Werther-like love just three years ago.

These affairs, however, belonged to his adolescence and left no more profound impression than they had aroused in the pretty young ladies.

In Vienna Beethoven was always involved in a love affair, at least as long I lived there, and sometimes made conquests which could have been very difficult indeed, if not impossible, for many an Adonis.

Whether one could have composed *Adelaide* and *Fidelio* and many other things without knowing love in its innermost depths, I leave to the judgment of experts and amateurs. But what can be clearer than Beethoven's statement in this letter as to how essential love was to him.[30]

I should also mention that, as far as I know, each of his loves was of much higher social standing than he.

(5) The von Breuning family had long occupied one of the highest positions in the Teutonic Order. Stephan's great-grandfather von Meirhoven was Chancellor of the Order; his successor to the office was Grandfather von Breuning, then the uncle, and finally the cousin. Stephan himself had been employed by the government in Mergentheim.

(6) The ill-feeling between these friends must have been considerable, since von Breuning was a music-lover, an excellent violinist trained by Ries's father, and himself had played in the Elector's chambers on several occasions.[31]

(7) Beethoven's assessment of his friend's well-being was only too correct. He rarely enjoyed sound health for long, but worked relentlessly all the same. He continued unflaggingly until his death on 4 June 1827, 2⅓ months after Beethoven's. Von Breuning was in every respect an excellent and widely respected man and his death is especially to be regretted since he was the only one who combined all the talents necessary to become Beethoven's biographer. With brief interruptions he had, after all, lived in intimate contact with him from the time he was ten until his death. As an indication of his high regard for von Breuning, Beethoven had also appointed him one of the two executors of his will.

***

In the meantime the correspondence between us was

not exactly very lively, as the next letter shows. I might have, even then, already mislaid some letters or perhaps given them to autograph collectors. At that time, still surrounded by a large number of people who had known Beethoven, I had no desire to collect his letters; every friend was a source of memories concerning him. And of course these were the accounts from secondary sources I mentioned in the foreword.

***

Vienna, 2 May 1810

Dear old friend — I can imagine that these lines of mine will occasion some astonishment — and yet, even though you have no written proof, you are still very much in my thoughts. — For a long time there has even been among my manuscripts one intended for you, which you will certainly receive this summer.(1) *For a couple of years now the quieter, calmer life has no longer been mine, and I have been forced to move in society. I have still not decided in favor of it, possibly more against it, but who is not affected by the storms all around him? Yet I would be happy, perhaps one of the happiest of men, if the demon had not settled in my ears. — If I had not read somewhere that man must not voluntarily part with his life as long as he can still perform a good deed, I would long ago have ceased to be — and, indeed, by my own hand. — Oh, life is so beautiful, but for me it is poisoned forever. —*

You will not refuse a friendly request if I ask you to obtain for me my baptismal certificate. — Whatever the expenses involved, maybe Steffen Breuning can pay you directly, since you have an account with him, and I will immediately reimburse Steffen here. — Should you consider it worth while to investigate the matter and if you would be willing to make the trip from

Coblenz to Bonn, then charge all the expenses to me. — There is one particular thing to watch out for, and that is: there was another brother born before me, but who died; he was also called Ludwig, though with the middle name Maria. To determine my age for certain you must first locate that Ludwig, then me; I do know that others have mistaken him for me and I have been said to be older than I am.(2) *Unfortunately, I have lived for some time without knowing myself how old I am. — I used to have a family register, but it has gotten lost, heaven knows how. — So please do not take it amiss if I urge you earnestly to find out all about Ludwig Maria and then the present Ludwig, who was born after him. — The sooner you send the baptismal certificate, the more indebted I shall be to you.*[32] *— I am told that you sing one of my songs in your Masonic Lodges, probably in E major, which I myself do not possess. Send it to me! I promise to recompense you three or four times over in some other way.*(3) *— Think of me kindly, however little I may seem to deserve it. — Embrace and kiss your dear wife, your children, everyone you hold dear — on behalf of your friend*

Beethoven.

(1) My lot in this respect was the same as that of his pupil Ries; the dedication remained in the letters. But are not they of higher value?

(2) A reference to an account by Ries, as it turned out later.

(3) Beethoven is wrong here; it was not a song especially composed by him of which he no longer had a copy; it was instead a different text using Beethoven's music of the *Opferlied* by Matthisson. I had done the same with a very early song composed by him: *Wer is ein freier Mann?* I have taken the liberty of placing these texts in the Appendix,[33] along with the vocal line and the text of an Adagio which was printed with

Beethoven's approval. Beethoven also requested a text to the theme of the variations which begin the grand sonata dedicated to Prince Lichnowsky (Opus 26), but I did not send it to him since I was not satisfied with it, nor with any other version.

Vienna, 29 September 1816

I am seizing this opportunity of reminding you of me through J. Simrock.(1) *— I hope you have received my copper engraving*(2) *and also the Bohemian glass. As soon as I travel through Bohemia once again, you will receive something like it again. All my best wishes. You are a husband, a father; so am I, but without a wife.*(3) *Give my greetings to all your family and our friends.*

Your friend, L. v. Beethoven.

Beethoven's portrait (1814) engraved from a drawing by Letronne

(1) Joseph Simrock, present owner of the business.

(2) *Dessiné — par — Letronne et gravé par — Hoefel. 1814.* At the bottom it says: For my friend Wegeler. Vienna, 27 March

1815. Ludw. van Beethoven. — Our mutual friend, the Director General of the Rhine Customs, Herr Eichhoff, brought it back for me from the Congress.

(3) Beethoven was educating the son of his brother Caspar who had died the previous year.

***

The letter below is written by another hand and only signed by Beethoven.

Vienna, 7 October 1826

My beloved old friend,

I cannot express what pleasure the letter from you and your Lorchen gave me. Of course the answer should have come back as quick as an arrow, but I am generally rather negligent in my correspondence because I think that the best people already know me well anyway. I compose an answer often in my head, but when I come to write it down, I usually throw my pen aside because I am not able to write as I feel. I remember all the love you have always shown me — for instance that time you had my room whitewashed, which was such a pleasant surprise.(1) *— The same with the Breuning family. If we drifted apart, it was simply the nature of circumstances. Each of us had to pursue his destiny and try to attain it. However, the eternally unshakeable principles of goodness have always bound us firmly and closely together. Unfortunately, I cannot write so much to you today as I would wish because I am confined to my bed and must restrict myself to answering a few points of your letter.*

You write that I am somewhere alleged to be a natural son of the late King of Prussia. That has also been said to me before, a long time ago. I have, however, made it a principle never to write anything about myself, nor to answer anything that is written about me. I therefore gladly leave it to you to make known to the world the integrity of my parents, and of my mother in particular. — You write about your son. It goes without saying that if he comes here, he will find a friend and father in me, and where I am in a position to be of any use to him or help him in any way, I will do so with pleasure.

I still have the silhouette of your Lorchen, which shows how much I still treasure all the love and kindness which surrounded me in my youth.(2)

Concerning my diplomas I would write only briefly that I am an honorary member of the Royal Society of Sciences in Sweden, as well as in Amsterdam, and I am also an honorary citizen of Vienna. — Recently a certain Dr. Spieker took my last grand symphony with choruses to Berlin; it is dedicated to the King, and I had to write the dedication in my own hand. I had previously requested permission from the Embassy to dedicate the work to the King, and this was granted. Dr. Spieker requested that I turn over the corrected manuscript to him myself, with emendations in my own hand, for presentation to the King, since it is to be placed in the Royal Library. There was also some mention of the Order of the Red Eagle, Second Class; whether anything will come of this, I do not know. I have never sought such honors, but at this age such an award would be rather welcome for various other reasons.

Incidentally, my motto has always been: Nulla dies sine linea, *and if I do let the Muse sleep, it is only that she may awake all the stronger.*(3) *I still hope to bring forth a few more great works into the world and then to finish my earthly course like an old child somewhere or other among kind people. — You will soon receive some music from the Schott Brothers in Mainz. — The portrait I am enclosing with this letter is indeed an artistic masterpiece, but it is not the latest done of me. — As for honors conferred on me — which, I know, give you pleasure — I must also report that the late King of France sent me a medal with the inscription:* Donné par le Roi à Monsieur Beethoven. *It was accompanied by an exceedingly courteous letter from the* Duc de Châtres, premier gentilhomme du Roi.[4]

My beloved friend! This will have to suffice for today. The memory of the past affects me anyway, and you receive this letter not without many tears. Now a start has been made, and soon you will have another letter from me. And the more often you write, the more pleasure you will give me. Our friendship precludes the need for questions on either side. My warmest regards. Please embrace and kiss your dear Lorchen and your children for me; and think of me then. God be with you all!

As always your true, faithful, and most respectful friend

Beethoven

(1) At the time Beethoven lived in the Peretti house in Wenzelgasse in Bonn.

(2) All the members of the von Breuning family and their closer friends had their silhouettes cut by the painter Neesen in Bonn over a period of two evenings. That is how I came into the possession of Beethoven's silhouette, which is reproduced here. Beethoven was probably then in his sixteenth year.

(3) On 24 July 1804 Beethoven wrote to Ries from Baden: "In all my life I would not have believed that I could be as lazy as I am here. If a burst of activity should follow, then it might really produce something worthwhile."

(4) What has been said about Beethoven's alleged indifference to, or even contempt of, such honors should be judged in this light.

Vienna, 17 February 1827[1]

My worthy old friend,

Fortunately I received at least your second letter from Breuning. I am still too weak to answer it, but you can imagine that everything it contained is welcome to me and what I wanted.[2] *My recovery, if I may call it that, is still progressing very slowly. I presume I must expect a fourth operation, although the doctors have said nothing about that yet. I remain patient and think: Occasionally some good may come of all that's evil. — But I was surprised, indeed, when I read in your last letter that you still had received nothing. — You will see from this letter that I had already written you by 10 December last year. The same applies to the portrait, as you will see from the date on it when you receive it.*[3] *— "Mrs. Steffen spoke."*[4] *— In short, Steffen asked that these things be sent to you when the opportunity arose, but they were left lying around until now, and really it was difficult enough to request their return before today. You will now receive the portrait by post through Messrs. Schott, who also forwarded the music to you. — There is so much I would still like to tell you today, but I am too weak; I can do no more than embrace you and your Lorchen in spirit. In true friendship and affection for you and yours,*

Your old devoted friend

Beethoven

This last letter was also written by another hand but signed by Beethoven.

(1) That is, one month before his death!

(2) If my memory serves me right, I had reminded him of Blumauer in my letter, who, once the water had been tapped, lived in good health for many years (see his letter to Stoll). I had told him of the plan to fetch him from the Bohemian baths, to take a few sidetrips with him along the upper Rhine, then down the Rhine to Coblenz, where he was to regain his strength completely, etc.

(3) Beethoven had written on the portrait above his name: "To my old, honored, beloved friend F. v. Wegeler." There is no date.
(4) The beginning of the second verse of the well-known song: "Zu Steffen sprach im Traume," etc.

⁂

The following are two letters from Beethoven to Fräulein von Breuning.

Vienna, 2 November 93

My adored Eleonore!
My dearest friend!

Only now, after I have lived for almost a whole year here in the capital, do you receive a letter from me, and yet you were surely always in my liveliest thoughts. I have often conversed in spirit with you and your dear family, although frequently not as calmly as I would have wished. Each time I recall that unfortunate quarrel, my behavior then seems most detestable. But it happened. How much would I give if I could but blot out of my life completely the way I behaved then, which so dishonored me and which was in complete contradiction to my character!(1) *There were of course many circumstances which kept us apart, and I believe the whisperings of third parties who passed on all that was said by both sides against the other was the main thing that prevented reconciliation. Each of us believed that we were speaking from absolute conviction, and yet it was no more than fanned-up anger, and we were both deceived. Your kind and noble nature, my dear friend, assures me that you have long since forgiven me. But they say that confession of one's own crime is the most sincere repentance; and that is what I wanted to do. — And now let us draw the curtain over the whole story and just learn from it the lesson that, when friends have quarrelled, it is always better not to use a mediator, but for one friend to go directly to the other.*

Here is a dedication to you from me, and I only wish the work greater and more worthy of you. They have been pestering me here to publish this little work, and I have taken the opportunity to give you, my very dear Eleonore, proof of my esteem and friendship for you and of my undying memory of your home. Accept this trifle and remember that it comes from a friend who admires you very much. Oh, if only it gives you pleasure, my wishes will be fulfilled.(2) *May it be a small remembrance of that time when I spent so many and such blissful hours in your home. Perhaps it will continue to remind you of me until I return one day — which, unfortunately, will not be for a long time. Oh, how happy we shall then be, my dear friend! You will then find your friend a more cheerful person; time and better fortune will have smoothed away the furrows on his brow etched by his earlier adverse lot.*

Should you see B. Koch(3)*, please tell her that it is not at all nice of her not to have written me even once. After all, I have written twice to her. I wrote three times to Malchus*(4) *and — no answer. Tell her that if she does not want to write, she should at least urge Malchus to. In concluding my letter I should like to venture one more request: I would like very much once again to possess a waistcoat of rabbit hair knitted by your hand, my dear friend.*(5) *Forgive your friend this presumptuous request. It springs from a great weakness for anything made by your hands. And between the two of us I might also add that there is a touch of vanity at the bottom of it too, namely, to be able to say that I possess something from one of the best, most admirable girls in Bonn. I still have, of course, the first waistcoat, which you had the great kindness to give me in Bonn, but fashion has made it so unfashionable that I can only keep it in my wardrobe as something from you and very dear to me.*

You would give me great pleasure if you would soon delight me with a friendly letter. Should my letters afford you pleasure, then I certainly promise to write faithfully, as much as it is within my power; I welcome every opportunity to show how very much I am

Your admiring

true friend

L. v. Beethoven

P.S. *The V. (variations) will be somewhat difficult to play, in particular the trills in the coda.*[6] *This should not frighten you. It is so arranged that you need not play anything but the trill; leave out the other notes; they are also in the violin part. I would never have written it that way, had I not often noticed that after I had been improvising of an evening, someone somewhere in Vienna would write down many of my own ideas the next day and go about boasting they were his.*[7] *Since I could expect that such things would appear soon, I decided to get ahead of them. There was also another reason: to embarrass the local pianists. Many of them are my mortal enemies, and I wanted to take my revenge on them in this way, because I knew full well that the V. would be placed in front of them here and there, and the gentlemen would then make a very poor showing.*

Beethoven

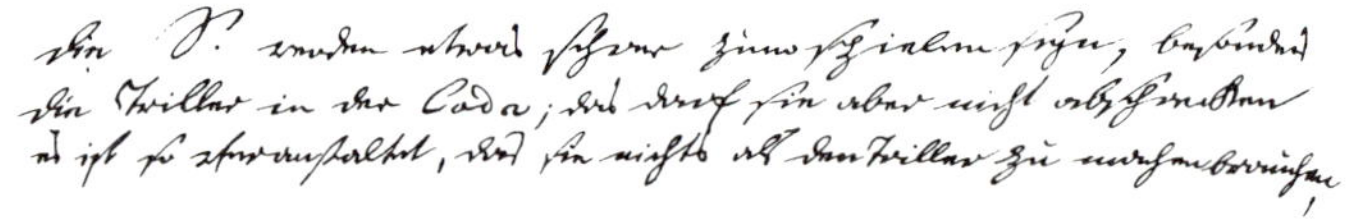

Excerpt from Beethoven's letter to Eleonore von Breuning, 2 Nov. 1793

(1) Compare what is said in note 4 to the first letter above, namely that Beethoven always begged forgiveness for more than he had committed.

(2) These are the variations on "Se vuol ballare" from Mozart's *Figaro*. In the Dunst edition, 4th section, No. 27.

Later a sonata, or rather sonatina, was also dedicated to her, which is No. 64 in the first section of the Dunst edition.[34]

(3) Barbara Koch from Bonn, later Countess Belderbusch, an intimate friend of Eleonore von Breuning, a lady who, of all the members of the female sex whom I came to know in the course of a rather long and eventful life, came closest to the ideal of a perfect woman. This claim is confirmed by all who were fortunate enough to know her well. She was surrounded not only by younger artists like Beethoven, the two Rombergs, Reicha, the twin brothers Kügelgen, and others, but also by intellectuals of all classes and ages, such as D. Crevelt, who lived in the same house, Professor Velten, who died young, Fishenich, later State Councilor, Professor, later Canon, Thaddäus Dereser, the future Bishop Wrede, Heckel and Floret, both private secretaries to the Elector, the private secretary of the Austrian Ambassador, Malchus, von Keverberg, subsequently Netherlands State Councilor, Hofrath von Bourscheidt, Christoph von Breuning, mentioned above, and many others. — Really, it was a wonderful, and in many ways lively time in Bonn while the personally gifted Elector Max Franz, Maria Theresa's youngest and favorite son, reigned there in peace.

(4) Subsequently Graf von Marienstadt, Minister of Finance in the Kingdom of Westphalia and later in the Kingdom of Würtemberg. Classical writer.

(5) Angora rabbits.

(6) A trill is continued over several bars with changing fingering, while the three other fingers are also occupied at

the same time. The fingering is marked.

(7) Beethoven complained to me about this kind of espionage. He named H. Ab.G.,[35] a most prolific composer of variations, who always took lodgings in his vicinity. This may have been one more reason why Beethoven always looked for lodgings on an open square or on the ramparts.

Elector Maximilian Franz (1756-1801)

Second letter to Fräulein von Breuning.[36]

I was most surprised by the beautiful cravat made by your own hand. Pleased though I was with the actual gift, still, it stirred sad feelings within me. It called up memories of bygone times, and a sense of shame as well, because you have treated me so generously. In truth, I did not think you still considered me worth remembering. Oh, if you could have seen how I felt when I received your gift, you would certainly not think I exaggerate when I tell you that your thoughtfulness made me weep; I was touched by sadness. — However little I may, in your eyes, deserve to be believed, I beg you, my friend (do still let me call you that!), to believe I have suffered greatly and am still suffering from the loss of your friendship. I will never forget you and your dear mother. You were so kind to me that your loss cannot and will not easily be restored; I know what I have lost and what you have been to me, but — were I to detail all this, I would have to return to scenes both unpleasant for you to hear and for me to describe.

As a small token of gratitude for remembering me so kindly, I am taking the liberty of sending you these variations and the rondo for one violin. I am very busy, otherwise I would have transcribed the sonata I promised you so long ago. In my manuscript it is little more than a sketch, and even someone as clever as Paraquin(1) *would have difficulty in copying it. You can have the rondo copied and then return the score to me. What I am sending you are the only things I have that might possibly suit your purposes. Besides, since you are now travelling to Kerpen*(2)*, I thought these trifles might perhaps give you some pleasure.*

Farewell, my friend — it is impossible for me to call you anything else, however indifferent you may be to me. Do believe that I continue to cherish you and your mother as much as ever. If I can contribute in any other way to your happiness, I beg you not to forget me. This is still the only means left for me to express my gratitude for the friendship I so enjoyed.

Have a happy journey and bring your dear mother back in full health again. Think occasionally of your true and devoted friend

Beethoven

Since this letter is without date and address and, moreover, starts at the very top of the page without the slightest spacing, I presume it is the third page of a letter whose first sheet has been lost. It demonstrates first of all the contention that Beethoven always apologized for more than he had committed and secondly his close relationship with the von Breuning family.

(1) A singer and double bass player in the Elector's orchestra, extremely reliable as an artist and highly respected as a man.

(2) An uncle of the von Breuning family lived in Kerpen. The family and their friends visited him on vacation every year for five or six weeks. Beethoven also spent some very happy weeks there several times and was often asked to play the organ.

***

From the letters of my brother-in-law Stephan von Breuning I would like to quote just one which is concerned with Beethoven's opera *Fidelio*.

Vienna, 2 June 1806

Dear Sister and dear Wegeler,

... If I remember correctly, I promised in my last letter to write you about Beethoven's opera. Since this will certainly interest you, I want to fulfill my promise. The music is among the most beautiful and perfect one could hope to hear; the subject is interesting because it concerns the liberation of a prisoner through the loyalty and courage of his wife. But nevertheless, probably nothing has caused so much aggravation for Beethoven as this work, whose worth will come to be fully appreciated only in the future. It was first performed seven days after the occupation by the French troops; in other words, at the most inopportune time. Naturally the theaters were empty, and Beethoven, who had also noticed some imperfections in the treatment of the text, withdrew the opera after three performances. After order was restored, he and I took it up again. I reworked the whole libretto for him, which made the action livelier and faster. He shortened many pieces and it was then performed three times

and was exceedingly well received. Then, however, his enemies at the theater got together and since he had offended several people, particularly during the second performance, they managed to prevent any further performances. Even before this they created many difficulties for him, of which one example may suffice. He could not even ensure that the second performance of the opera was announced under the new title Fidelio, *as it was also called in the French original, and under which it was printed after the changes had been made. Despite various promises the first title* Leonore *appeared on the announcement posters.*[37] *The conspiracy is all the more disagreeable for Beethoven since he was depending on payment derived from a percentage of the receipts. Now that the opera is no longer being performed, he has been set back somewhat in his financial affairs and will recover all the more slowly because he has lost a great deal of his desire and love for his work through the treatment he has received. I may well have given him the greatest pleasure then since completely without his knowledge I had a little poem printed and distributed in the theater in November as well as for the performance at the end of March. I shall copy them both for Wegeler here, for I know from former times that he sets store by such things, and since at one time I composed verses on his investment as* Rector magnificus celeberrimae universitatis Bonnensis, *he can now see by comparison whether my talent for occasion poetry has made any progress. The first little poem was in unrhymed iambics:*

> *We hail thee now; thou trav'lest noble paths;*
> *Applause of connoisseurs dost spur thee on.*
> *Thy modesty restrained thee much too long.*
> *Though thou hast but begun, the prize is thine*
> *And older warriors gladly welcome thee.*
> *Thy dazzling sound has glory, strength, and depth —*
> *A golden river flowing rich and full.*
> *In perfect union skill and grace entwine.*
> *Thy vital soul taught thee to touch mankind.*

Our hearts were stirred, elated, pierced in turn
By Leonore's courage, love, and tears;
Now jub'lant echoes vie to praise her faith
And dread anxiety gives way to bliss.
Press on; be brave; pour out triumphant sound.
Awestruck posterity will wonder were
There ever other wonders in the world.

The second consists of two stanzas and contains a reference to the presence of the French troops at the time of the opera's first performance:

We hail thee once again upon this course
Where thou embark'st in anxious fearful times
When dreadful truth ripped down the beauteous veil
Of sweet illusive dreams, and all were cast
In turbulence, as when a fragile ship
Is flung from wave to wave on angry seas;
Art fled in fear from cruel scenes of war,
Nor did we weep from tenderness, but woe.

Thy mighty stride must bring us to our feet,
Thy holy vision raise our eyes on high
Where thou hast seen pure art and feeling wed.
With golden wreaths the muse has crowned thy brow,
While from the laurel grove Apollo smiles
And consecrates, himself, your deity.
Long may you reign! For in your music pure
Is heard eternal beauty's pow'r and grace.

Copying this has really tired me out completely, so I shall close this letter which is rather long anyway. I want to tell you just one more bit of news — Lichnowsky has sent the opera to the Queen of Prussia and I hope that the performances in Berlin might just show the Viennese the worth of what they have at home.† [37a]

† [Translator's note: The English translation of these and other poems in this volume are not meant to be literally exact, but to reflect the spirit and tone of the originals.]

Appendix

Words set to Beethoven's music for Mathisson's *Opferlied* (page 46).

On the Initiation of a Mason

Commence the task! With sacred fire
Exalt in youth the firm desire
    For worthy work concluded;
Give strength to weakness; make weak youth believe
He will the highest goals achieve
    The victor's palm included.

Root from his soul all but the Truth.
Ensure, great Lord, that our brave youth
    With righteous men will wander.
Oh grant he will find favor in your eyes.
Urge him and his companions wise,
    The Mason's life to ponder.

* * *

Words set to the song: *Wer ist ein freier Mann?* (page 46)

Masonic Questions

Chorus: What is the Mason's goal?
A Voice: With noble purpose striving
On higher plains arriving
Set free from Chance's role
Chorus: That is the Mason's goal,
The Mason's splendid goal.

What marks the Mason's bond?
Through thought and deed deserving
Humanity preserving
On earth and then beyond
That marks the Mason's bond,
The Mason's holy bond.

To whom are Masons drawn?
Men comforting and giving
By habit selfless living
And ruled by heart, not brawn,
To such are Masons drawn
They willingly are drawn.

Whom does a Mason scorn?
Those weak and yielding ever
Those heeding conscience never
Abject, like beasts, forlorn
They earn the Mason's scorn
The Mason's deepest scorn.

What weighs on Masons' hearts?
Each tear still daily flowing,
Each life that should be growing
That misery imparts
That weighs on Masons' hearts
On Masons' feeling hearts.

When does his heart beat glad?
When in our grand tradition,
Not asking recognition,
He makes the world less sad.
Then does his heart beat glad
His heart beat warm and glad.

Who praises Masons' deeds?
Our end and our beginning
Who set the planets spinning
And answers all our needs,
He praises Masons' deeds,
The Masons' noble deeds.

In the Dunst edition, 4th section, No. 27.

⁂

The Elegy

Voice line and words set to the Adagio from the first of the three sonatas dedicated to J. Haydn (*Opus 2*) with the inscription: Elegy. This arrangement appears in the edition of Beethoven's work erroneously identified as a composition unified from its inception. (See the musical illustration at page 143)

(These three poems were composed in 1797.)

PART TWO

Ferdinand Ries (1784-1838)

Foreword

My friend Wegeler has frequently urged me to collect a few incidents from the life of my immortal teacher and affectionate friend Beethoven and, should I not wish to make other arrangements, to publish the material jointly with some of his reminiscences. So I have been persuaded, not without a certain feeling of anxiety, to set down a few particularly memorable recollections and to place these notes, as well as some of Beethoven's letters, of which I possess a large number, at the disposal of my friend for him to use as he sees fit.* The truth of the facts recorded here and the fame of the man whom they concern should alone lend value to these notes. My remarks should serve as a continuation and an elaboration of the preceding notes by my friend Wegeler, and our mutual endeavors should form, as we intend, a genuine source on which a complete biography of our immortal friend can be based. The plainness of style will, I hope, be graciously overlooked, since hitherto I have communicated with the public only through musical compositions. The same goes for a possible lack of order in presentation. I shall relate the events as they occur to me; should the reader be of a mind to do so, he will find it easy enough to put them in order. And so without further ado I will begin.

Frankfurt/Main, December 1837.

---

* A comment by the author of the article on Ferdinand Ries in the *Conversations-Lexicon der neuesten Zeit* was a strong incentive for me to encourage my friend to collect these reminiscences. The writer remarked: "The accounts which Ries could give about his close relationship with Beethoven are fascinating, particularly since his contact with the Master not only covers the period when the composer rose to the highest peak of his creative power, but also includes that time when Beethoven had the misfortune to lose his hearing. The Beethoven biographies and his literary remains contain all too little about the psychological effect of this tragedy on the great man, and we possess so few detailed reports on his character, on his method and habit of composition, that it would be especially appropriate for Ries to publish his memoirs of that remarkable period."

Wegeler.

From my father I received my first, and most fortunately for my whole career, very thorough instruction on the piano and in music in general. When he decided that it was time for me to continue my studies abroad, since Bonn had suffered greatly because of the war, I was sent to Munich and then to Vienna at the age of fifteen.

My father's friendly relationship with Beethoven as a boy and as a young man justified the expectation that I would be well received by him. A letter of recommendation introduced me. When I presented it to Beethoven on my arrival in Vienna in 1800,[38] he was intensely occupied with the completion of his oratorio *Christ on the Mount of Olives*, since this was due to receive its first performance in a great Academy concert in the Wiener Theater, an event very advantageous to him. He read the letter through and said: "I cannot answer your father now; but write to him that I have not forgotten how my mother died; he will be satisfied with that." Later I learned that my father had been active in supporting him in every way on that occasion, since the family was in great want.

⁂

Right from the very first few days Beethoven found that he was able to make use of me, and thus I was frequently called as early as five in the morning, as indeed happened on the day the oratorio was to be performed. I found him in bed, writing on single sheets of paper. When I asked him what they were, he answered: "Trombones." — The trombones played from these manuscript pages at the performance.

Had these parts been forgotten in copying? Were they an afterthought? I was still too young at the time to give any thought to questions of such artistic interest. Presumably it was an afterthought, though, since Beethoven would probably have had in his possession the uncopied sheets, as well as those which had been copied. The rehearsal began at eight o'clock in the morning and, beside the oratorio, the following new things were also performed for the first time: Beethoven's Second Symphony in D Major, the Piano Concerto in C Minor and yet another new piece which I do not remember. It was a dreadful rehearsal, and by half past two everyone was exhausted and more or less dissatisfied.

Prince Karl Lichnowsky, who attended the rehearsal from the beginning, had bread and butter, cold meat, and wine brought in great baskets.[39] He most graciously invited everyone to help themselves, which everyone eagerly did, and a general good humor was restored. The Prince then asked that the oratorio be rehearsed once more so that everything might go really well in the evening and that the first work of this type by Beethoven might be presented to the public in a manner worthy of it. The rehearsal was therefore resumed. The concert began at six o'clock, but it was so long that a couple of the pieces were not performed.

There was something most striking about the *Larghetto quasi andante* of the Symphony in D just mentioned; which Beethoven had presented to me in a score in his own hand, out of pure friendship (and which was unfortunately stolen from me by a friend). This *Larghetto* is so beautifully, so purely and happily conceived and the melodic line so natural that one can hardly imagine anything in it was ever changed. The design was indeed from the beginning as it is now. However, in the second violins, almost in the very first lines, a most significant part of the accompaniment was changed in many places and at some points also in the violas. But everything is so carefully crossed out that I could never discover the original idea despite great effort. I also questioned Beethoven about it, who retorted drily: "It is better this way."

⁂

In 1802[40] Beethoven composed his Third Symphony (now known as the *Sinfonia eroica*) in Heiligenstadt, a village one and a half hours outside Vienna.

Heiligenstadt c. 1821

When he was composing, Beethoven frequently had a certain subject in mind, even though he often laughed at and inveighed against descriptive music, particularly the frivolous sort. Occasionally Haydn's *Creation* and *The Seasons* came under fire in this respect, though Beethoven did recognize Haydn's greater achievements, especially the many choral works and certain other things for which he properly lavished praise on Haydn. In this symphony Beethoven had thought about Bonaparte during the period when he was still First Consul. At that time Beethoven held him in the highest regard and compared him to the greatest Roman consuls. I myself, as well as many of his close friends, had seen this symphony, already copied in full score, lying on his table. At the very top of the title page stood the word "Buonaparte" and at the very bottom "Luigi van Beethoven," but not a word more. Whether and with what the intervening space was to be filled I do not know. I was the first to tell him the news that Bonaparte had declared himself emperor, whereupon he flew into a rage and shouted: "So he too is nothing more than an ordinary man. Now he also will trample all human rights underfoot, and only pander to his own ambition; he will place himself above everyone else and become a tyrant!" Beethoven went to the table, took hold of the title page at the top, ripped it all the way through, and flung it on the floor. The first page was written anew and only then did the symphony receive the title *Sinfonia eroica*. Prince Lobkowitz later bought this composition from Beethoven for his own use for several years, and it was performed many times at his palace. Here it happened that Beethoven, who was himself conducting, once threw the whole orchestra out of rhythm in the second part of the first *Allegro*, where it runs on so long in half-notes on the off-beat, that they had to start all over again from the beginning.

⁂

In that same *Allegro* Beethoven plays the horn a mean trick. Several bars before the theme re-enters completely in the second part, Beethoven has the horn suggest it, while the two violins are still holding a chord on the second. To anyone who does not know the score it inevitably gives the impression that the horn player has miscounted and entered too early. During the first rehearsal of this symphony, which went appallingly, the horn player did come in correctly. I was standing next to Beethoven and believing the entry wrong said: "That damned horn player! Can't he count? — It sounds terrible!" I believe I was very close indeed to having my ears boxed. — Beethoven was a long time in forgiving me.

⁂

That same night Beethoven played his Quintet for piano and wind instruments; the famous oboist Ram from Munich played also and joined Beethoven in the quintet. — In the last Allegro a pause occurs several times before the theme begins again; in one of these pauses Beethoven suddenly started improvising, taking the Rondo as his theme, and entertained himself and his listeners for quite some time, although the other players were not so amused. They were annoyed and Mr. Ram was even angry. It did indeed look rather comic to see these gentlemen, expecting to begin any moment, constantly raising their instruments to their mouths, only to put them down quietly again. At last Beethoven was satisfied and returned to the Rondo. The whole company was enchanted.

⁂

The funeral march in A flat minor in the sonata dedicated to Prince Lichnowsky (Opus 26) originated in the great praise Paer's funeral march in his opera *Achilles* received from Beethoven's friends.*

⁂

When the immensely famous Steibelt came from Paris to Vienna, several of Beethoven's friends were worried lest he should cast a shadow on Beethoven's reputation.[42] Steibelt did not visit him; they met for the first time one evening in the house of Count Fries, where Beethoven gave his new trio in B flat major for piano, clarinet, and cello (Opus 11) its initial performance. This work offers the pianist no opportunity to display his virtuosity. Steibelt listened with a certain condescension, paid Beethoven a few compliments, and felt confident of his own superiority. — He played a quintet of his

* Beethoven was in a box with a lady who was very dear to him when *La Molinara* was being performed. During the famous "Nel cuor piu non mi sento" the lady said that she had once had variations on this theme, but had lost them. During the night Beethoven wrote VI variations on the aria and sent them to the lady the next morning with the inscription, *Variazioni*, etc. *perdute par la — — ritrovate par Luigi van Beethoven.* They are so easy that they were presumably intended for the lady to sight-read.

Wglr.[41]

own composition, improvised, and produced a great effect with his *tremulandos*, which were something quite new then. Beethoven could not be persuaded to play again. A week later there was another concert at Count Fries. Steibelt again played a quintet with much success, but more important (one could sense this) he had prepared a brilliant improvisation, choosing the identical theme on which the variations in Beethoven's trio were written. This outraged Beethoven's admirers as well as Beethoven himself. It was now his turn to improvise at the piano. He seated himself in his usual, I might say unmannerly, fashion at the instrument, almost as if he had been pushed. He had picked up the cello part of Steibelt's quintet on his way to the piano, and placing it upside down on the music rack (intentionally?), he hammered out a theme from the first few bars with one finger. — Insulted and irritated as he was, he improvised in such a manner that Steibelt left the room before Beethoven had finished, never wanted to meet him again, and even made it a condition that Beethoven not be invited when his own company was desired.

Beethoven almost always postponed the composition of the majority of his works due by a certain date until the very last moment. He had, for instance, promised Ponto,[43] the famous horn player, that he would compose a sonata (Opus 17) for piano and horn and would play it with him at a concert given by Ponto. The concert with the sonata was announced, but the sonata was not yet started. On the day before the performance Beethoven began the work and had it ready for the concert.

⁂

Beethoven had originally written the famous Sonata for Violin in A minor[44] (Opus 47), dedicated to Rudolph Kreuzer in Paris, for an English artist named Bridgetower. Matters were not much better in this case, either, even though a large part of the first Allegro was ready in plenty of time. Bridgetower began to put a great deal of pressure on Beethoven, since his concert was already arranged and he wanted to practice his part. One morning Beethoven had me called at half past four and said: "Copy the violin part of the first Allegro for me quickly." — (His usual copyist was already hard at work.) The piano part was only sketched in here and there. The particularly beautiful theme with variations in F major Bridgetower had to play from Beethoven's own manuscript at his concert in the Augarten at eight in the morning, because there was no time to copy it.

On the other hand, the violin and piano parts of the last 6/8 Allegro in A major were very beautifully copied because it had originally belonged to the first sonata with violin (Opus 30) in A major, dedicated to the Emperor Alexander. Beethoven later substituted the present variations, because the other movement was too brilliant for this sonata.

***

Beethoven gave a grand Academy concert in the Theater an der Wien, where his C minor and Pastoral Symphonies (the fifth and the sixth) together with his Fantasy for Piano with Orchestra and Chorus were performed for the first time. In the last work the clarinetist inadvertently took a repeat of eight bars just where the last cheerful theme begins its variation. Since there were only a few instruments playing, this mistake was naturally all the more grating to the ear. Beethoven jumped up in anger, turned round, and abused the orchestra members in the coarsest manner so loudly that the whole audience heard it. Finally he shouted: "From the beginning!" The theme began again, everyone made their correct entrances, and it was a splendid success.[45] When the concert was over, however, the artists recalled all too vividly the sarcastic names Beethoven had publicly bestowed upon them and flew into the greatest rage, as though the insult had only just happened. They swore they would never play again if Beethoven were with the orchestra, etc. This lasted until he had composed something new again, when their curiosity overcame their anger.

***

A similar scene is supposed to have occurred on another occasion. This time, however, the orchestra made him feel his injustice more forcefully and insisted in all seriousness that he not conduct. Beethoven then had to stay in an adjoining room during the rehearsal and it took a very long time before the dispute was straightened out again.

***

Of all composers Beethoven thought most highly of Mozart and Handel, followed by S. Bach. If I found him with music in his hand, or if anything lay on his desk, it was sure to be a composition by one of these heroes. Haydn rarely got away without a few digs. Beethoven's grudge here probably went back to earlier days. The following tale may account for one reason. Beethoven's three trios (Opus 1) were to be introduced to the music world in a soirée at Prince Lichnowsky's. Most of Vienna's artists and music lovers had been invited, above all Haydn, whose opinion was anxiously awaited by everyone. The trios were played and caused a tremendous stir. Haydn, too, said many fine things about them but advised Beethoven not to publish the third one in C minor. This astonished Beethoven, since he considered it the best, and in fact to this day it is always found to be most pleasing and has the greatest effect. Haydn's remark of course made an unpleasant impression on Beethoven, leaving him with a feeling that Haydn was envious and jealous and did not wish him well. I must admit that I did not really believe Beethoven when he told me this. I therefore later took the opportunity to ask Haydn himself about it. His answer confirmed Beethoven's story in that he said he had not imagined that this trio would be so quickly and easily understood nor so favorably received by the public.

⁂

On the same occasion I asked Haydn why he had never written a violin quintet and received the laconic answer that he had always found four voices sufficient. I was actually told that Haydn had been asked for three quintets but that he could never compose them because he had become so accustomed to the quartet style that he could not find the fifth voice. He had started, but one attempt turned into a quartet, another into a sonata.

***

Haydn had wished Beethoven to put on the title page of his first works "Pupil of Haydn." Beethoven did not want to do that because, as he said, he had had some instruction from Haydn but had never learned anything from him. (During his first stay in Vienna Beethoven had received some lessons from Mozart, but, he complained, Mozart had never played for him.) Beethoven had also taken lessons in counterpoint from Albrechtsberger and in dramatic music from Salieri. I knew them all well; all three thought very highly of Beethoven but were of one opinion of him as a student. Each said Beethoven was always so stubborn and so bent on having his own way that he had had to learn many things through hard experience which he had refused earlier to accept through instruction. Albrechtsberger and Salieri in particular were of this opinion. The former's pedantic rules and the latter's trivial ones concerning dramatic composition (following the Italian school of the time) could not appeal to Beethoven. Whether the studies published by Ritter von Seyfried furnish irrefutable proof that Beethoven, during his two years of apprenticeship under the eyes of Albrechtsberger, devoted himself to theoretical studies with indefatigable perseverance therefore remains open to doubt.[46]

***

What follows may serve to corroborate the above. Once during a walk together I mentioned two perfect fifths which resound noticeably and beautifully in one of his first string quartets in C minor. Beethoven did not remember them and claimed that it was wrong to call them fifths. Since he was in the habit of always carrying music paper with him, I asked for a sheet of it and wrote down the passage for him with all four voices. When he saw that I was right, he said: "Well, and who has forbidden them?" Since I did not know how to take that question, he repeated it several times, until, very taken aback, I finally answered: "Well, it is one of the very first basic principles." The question was again repeated, whereupon I said: "Marpurg, Kirnberger, Fuchs, etc., etc., all the theoreticians!" "Well, I allow them!" was his answer.[47]

***

Beethoven had promised the three solo sonatas (Opus 31) to Nägeli in Zurich, while his brother Carl (Caspar), who unfortunately always meddled in the business arrangements, wanted to sell these sonatas to a publisher in Leipzig. There were frequent altercations between the brothers over this, because Beethoven wanted to honor his promise. When the sonatas were ready to be sent off, Beethoven was living in Heiligenstadt. During a walk the brothers quarreled again, eventually coming to blows. On the next day he gave me the sonatas, to send to Zurich immediately, as well as a letter to his brother which was enclosed within another letter to

Stephan von Breuning, meant for his brother's perusal. No one could have preached a more beautiful sermon in a more kind-hearted way than did Beethoven to his brother about his behavior of the day before. First he showed him the true, despicable character of his conduct, then forgave him completely, but also predicted a miserable future for him if he did not radically change his life and behavior. The letter which he sent to Breuning was also exquisitely written.

***

Those same sonatas occasioned another unusual incident. When the proofs arrived, I found Beethoven busy writing. "Play the sonatas through for me," he said, while he remained sitting at his writing desk. There were an uncommon number of mistakes in the proofs, which made Beethoven very impatient indeed. At the end of the first Allegro in the Sonata in G major, however, Nägeli had even included four measures of his own composition, after the fourth beat of the last firmata:

When I played these, Beethoven jumped up in a rage, ran over, and all but pushed me from the piano, shouting:

"Where the devil does it say that?" — His astonishment and anger can hardly be imagined when he saw it printed that way. I was told to draw up a list of all the errors and to send the sonatas immediately to Simrock in Bonn who was to reprint them and add, *Edition très correcte*.[48] — This designation still stands on the title page. The four measures, however, are still to be found in several of the subsequent editions.

Nikolaus Simrock (1752-1833)

The following notes written to me by Beethoven belong in this context:

Be so kind as to correct the mistakes and send a list of the errors to Simrock immediately with a note telling him he should see to it that these be published soon. — I will send him the sonata and the concerto the day after tomorrow.

Beethoven

I must ask you once again to undertake the disagreeable job of making a clean copy of the Zurich sonatas with the mistakes corrected and to send it to Simrock; you will find the list of mistakes which you prepared in my rooms at the Wieden.

Dear Ries! The marks are badly indicated and also the notes are transposed in several instances — please do pay more attention! — otherwise the work is again all in vain. Ch'a detto l'amato bene?

⁂

Beethoven arranged an engagement for me as pianist with Count Browne. The Count spent some time in Baden near Vienna, where for a group of enthusiastic Beethoven fans I frequently had to play Beethoven's compositions in the evenings, partly from the music, partly by heart. Here I became convinced that for most people the name alone is enough for them to find everything in a work beautiful and admirable, or mediocre and inferior. One day, tired of playing by heart, I played a march which I made up as I went along without giving it any further thought. An old countess, who was really plaguing Beethoven with her devotion, went into ecstasies over it, since she believed it to be something new by him. I readily went along with this idea, making fun both of her and the other enthusiasts. As ill luck would have it, Beethoven himself came to Baden the next day. He had hardly entered the room at Count Browne's when the old lady began rattling on about the exceptionally magnificent march which bore the stamp of genius. Imagine my embarrassment! Knowing full well that Beethoven could not stand the old countess, I quickly pulled him aside and whispered to him how I had only wanted to make fun of her foolishness. Luckily he took the matter very well, but my embarrassment grew when I had to repeat the march, which this time turned out much worse, with Beethoven standing beside me. He then received from everyone the most extravagant praise for his genius, to which he listened in utter confusion and anger, until at last he dissolved into roaring laughter. Later he said to me: "There you see, my dear Ries! Those are the great connoisseurs who aspire to judge all music so correctly and astutely. Just give them the name of their darling; more than that they do not need."

⁂

This march, incidentally, did have the positive result that Count Browne immediately commissioned from Beethoven the composition of three marches for four hands, which were dedicated to the Princess Esterhazy (Opus 45).[49]

⁂

Beethoven composed part of the second march while — this still seems unbelievable to me — giving me a lesson on a sonata which I was to perform in the evening at a small concert in the Count's house. I was also to play the marches there with him.

While we were playing these duets, the young Count P. . . .[50] spoke so loudly and freely with a beautiful lady in the doorway to the next room that, after several attempts to restore silence had proved futile, Beethoven suddenly pulled my hand away from the piano in the middle of the piece, jumped up, and said very loudly: "I will not play for such swine."

All attempts to bring him back to the piano failed; he would not even permit me to play the sonata. This, to everyone's displeasure, put an end to the evening's music.

⁂

One evening at Count Browne's I was to play a Beethoven sonata (A minor, Opus 23), a work not often heard. Since Beethoven was present and I had never studied this sonata with him, I declared myself willing to play any other sonata, but not that one. Beethoven was then approached and finally said: "Well, you will surely not play it so badly that I cannot listen to it," and so I was obliged to play it. As usual, Beethoven turned pages for me. At a leap in the left hand, where one particular note must be brought out, I missed the note completely, and Beethoven tapped me on the head with one finger. Princess L. . . . .,[51] who sat leaning against the piano facing me, noticed this with a smile. When I had finished, Beethoven said: "Very good. You did not need to study this sonata with me first. The finger-tap was just meant to prove that I was paying attention." Later that evening Beethoven was also obliged to play and chose the D Minor Sonata (Opus 31), which had just been published.[52] The Princess, who probably expected that Beethoven too would make a mistake somewhere, now stood behind his chair while I turned pages. In bars 53 to 54 Beethoven missed the entry, and instead of descending two notes and then two more, he struck each quarter note in the descending passage with his whole hand (three or four notes at once). It sounded as if the piano was being cleaned. The Princess rapped him several times on the head, not at all delicately, saying: "If the pupil receives one tap of the finger for one missed note, then the Master must be punished with a full hand for worse mistakes." Everyone laughed, Beethoven most of all. He started again and performed marvelously. The Adagio in particular was incomparably played.

*
**

Many of Beethoven's compositions appeared with the notation *Arrangé par l'Auteur même*, but only four of these are genuine: from his famous septet he arranged (1) a violin quintet and (2) a piano trio; from his quintet for piano and four wind instruments he arranged (3) the quartet for piano and string trio; he also arranged (4) the violin concerto (Opus 61) dedicated to Stephen von Breuning as a piano concerto. Many other things were arranged by me, checked through by Beethoven, and then sold by his brother Caspar under Beethoven's name.[52a]

*
**

When Beethoven gave me lessons, I must say that contrary to his nature he was extraordinarily patient. I could only attribute this, and his almost unfailingly amicable behavior toward me, mainly to his love and affection for my father. Thus he sometimes made me repeat a thing ten times or even more often. In the Variations in F major, dedicated to Princess Odescalchi (Opus 34), I had to repeat the last Adagio variations entirely seventeen times. Still he was not satisfied with the expression in the little cadenza, even though I thought I had played it just as well as he did. I received nearly two full hours of instruction that day. If I made a mistake somewhere in a passage, or struck wrong notes, or missed intervals — which he often wanted strongly emphasized — he rarely said anything. However, if I lacked expression in crescendos, etc. or in the character of a piece, he became angry because, he maintained, the first was accident, while the latter resulted from inadequate knowledge, feeling, or attention. The first happened quite frequently to him, too, even when he played in public.

⁂

Beethoven was extremely good natured, but he was also easily irritated or quick to be suspicious. This was caused in part by his deafness but even more so by the behavior of his brothers. Any stranger could freely slander his most loyal friends, since he believed everything all too quickly and unconditionally. He would then neither reproach the victim nor demand an explanation but would immediately show the greatest insolence and contempt in his behavior toward him. Since he was extremely passionate in everything he did, he also looked for the most vulnerable side of the supposed enemy to show his anger. Therefore one frequently did not know how one stood with him until the matter was cleared up, usually by accident. Then, however, he always tried to compensate for the injustice he had done as quickly and effectively as possible. From among many instances I have chosen the following incidents as proof of this.

Beethoven was to become Kapellmeister at the court of the King of Westphalia. The contract, ensuring him six hundred ducats salary besides (unless I am mistaken) a carriage at his disposal, had been drawn up and awaited only his signature. The Archduke Rudolph and the Princes Lobkowitz and Kinsky countered this offer with the guarantee of a salary for life under the sole condition that he remain within the Empire. I knew of the first arrangement but not of the second offer when suddenly Kapellmeister Reichard came to me and said Beethoven would certainly not accept the position in Cassel; wouldn't I, as Beethoven's only pupil, like to go there at a smaller salary. I did not believe him and immediately went to Beethoven to inquire as to the truth of the matter and to ask his advice. For three weeks I was refused admittance; even my letters remained unanswered. Finally I saw Beethoven at a fancy ball. I immediately approached him and acquainted him with the reason for my request, whereupon he said in a cutting tone: "So — you think you could fill a position that was offered to me?" — He then remained cold and shunned me. The next morning I went to him to explain the misunderstanding. His servant told me in a rude tone that his master was not at home, even though I heard him singing and playing in the next room. Realizing that the servant had no intention of announcing me, I decided to go straight in anyway, but the fellow jumped for the door and shoved me away. This infuriated me. I grabbed him by the throat and roughly threw him to the floor. Beethoven, alarmed by the tumult, came running out, found the servant still on the floor and me pale as death. Absolutely distraught by this point, I deluged him with such vehement reproaches that he was speechless with astonishment and just stood there, immobile. When the whole misunderstanding was cleared up, Beethoven said: "I did not know it was like that; I had been told you tried to get the position behind my back." Upon my assurance that I had not responded to the offer at all, he immediately went out of his way with me to make good his injustice. However, it was too late; I did not receive the position, even though it would have been very advantageous for me at the time.[53]

His brothers went to great lengths to keep all close friends away from him. It did not matter how badly they behaved toward him (if one were able to convince Beethoven of this at all); they needed only to shed a few tears and he immediately forgot everything. He then used to say: "He is, after all, my brother," and the friend would be reproached for his solicitude and frankness.* The brothers eventually had their own way in that many friends retreated from him,

* Von Seyfried wrote: "Two younger brothers had followed him to Vienna and lifted from his shoulders the oppressive burden of worrying about his economic needs. They really found it necessary to act as guardians for this high priest of art, who was virtually a total stranger to ordinary life." Just how that remark is to be taken must be left to the reader's discretion.

Wglr.

especially when his deafness made it increasingly difficult to converse with him.

***

Beethoven's hearing began to suffer as early as 1802, but the trouble disappeared for a time.* He was so sensitive to the onset of his deafness that one had to be very careful not to make him feel the disability by talking loudly. If he had not understood something, he usually blamed it on his absent-mindedness, which was indeed a strongly developed trait. Much of the time he lived in the country, where I often went to take a lesson from him. Occasionally he would say at eight in the morning after breakfast: "Let us go for a little walk first." So we would go for a walk, often not returning until three or four o'clock, after we had eaten something in one of the villages. On one of these outings Beethoven gave me the first startling proof of his loss of hearing, which Stephan von Breuning had already mentioned to me. I called his attention to a shepherd in the forest who was playing most pleasantly on a flute cut from lilac wood. For half an hour Beethoven could not hear anything at all and became extremely quiet and gloomy, even though I repeatedly assured him that I did not hear anything any longer either (which was, however, not the

---

* His first and second letters to me show that he suffered even earlier than 1800 from this malady, which he confided to me as his friend and as a doctor, but managed to conceal even from his closer associates for several years.

Wglr.

case). — When at times he did seem in good spirits, he often became actually boisterous. However, this happened very rarely.

⁂

During a similar walk we went so far astray that we didn't get back to Döbling, where Beethoven lived, until nearly eight o'clock. The entire way he had hummed, or sometimes even howled, to himself — up and down, up and down, without singing any definite notes. When I asked what this was, he replied: "A theme for the last Allegro of the sonata has occurred to me" (in F minor, Opus 57). When we entered the room he rushed to the piano without taking off his hat. I took a seat in the corner and he soon forgot all about me. He stormed on for at least an hour with the new finale of this sonata, which is so beautiful. Finally he got up, was surprised to see me still there, and said: "I cannot give you a lesson today. I still have work to do."[54]

⁂

Among pianists he praised only one to me as an excellent player: John Cramer. All the others found little favor with him. He was most reluctant to play his own things.

Once he seriously planned a grand tour with me, where I was to arrange all the concerts and play his piano concerti and other compositions. He himself wanted only to conduct and to improvise. His improvising was, of course, the most extraordinary thing one could ever hear, especially when he was in a good mood or was irritated. All the artists I ever heard improvise did not come anywhere near the heights reached by Beethoven in this discipline. The wealth of ideas which poured forth, the moods to which he surrendered himself, the variety of interpretation, the complicated challenges which evolved or which he introduced were inexhaustible.

⁂

One day when we were talking about themes for fugues after the lesson was over, I sat at the piano and he sat down beside me. I played the theme of the first fugue from Graun's *Death of Jesus*. He began to imitate it with his left hand, then added a voice with his right hand, and continued on without the slightest interruption for a good half hour. I still cannot understand how he managed to remain in such an uncomfortable position for so long. His own enthusiasm rendered him insensible to external conditions.

⁂

When Clementi came to Vienna, Beethoven wanted to call on him at once; his brother, however, put it into his head that Clementi had to visit him first. Clementi, despite the fact that he was much older, would probably have done this anyway, if some gossip about it had not arisen. So it came about that Clementi was in Vienna for a long time without knowing Beethoven other than by sight. We frequently ate lunch at the same table at the Swan, Clementi with his pupil Klengel[55] and

Beethoven with me. Everyone knew who everyone was, but no one spoke with each other or even nodded a greeting. The two pupils had to imitate their masters, because presumably each one risked losing his lessons otherwise. I certainly would have suffered that, since with Beethoven compromises were never possible.

⁂

Originally there had been a grand Andante in the sonata (C major, Opus 53) dedicated to his first patron, the Count Waldstein. A friend of Beethoven's suggested to him that the sonata was too long, whereupon he was taken to task most severely. Calmer deliberation, however, soon convinced my teacher that the remark had some truth to it. He then published the grand Andante in F Major, in 3/8 time,[56] on its own and later composed the interesting introduction to the rondo in its present form.

⁂

This Andante, however, left me with a sad memory. When Beethoven first played it for our friend Krumpholz[57] and me, we liked it enormously and pestered him until he repeated it. On the way home I passed the house of Prince Lichnowsky, and I stopped in to tell him about Beethoven's marvelous new composition. I was compelled to play the piece as best I could remember. Since I kept remembering more of it, the Prince entreated me to repeat it. So it happened that he, too, learned part of it.

To surprise Beethoven, the Prince went to him the next day and told him that he too had composed something, which was not at all bad. Despite Beethoven's firm statement that he did not want to hear it, the Prince sat down and to the composer's astonishment played a good portion of his own Andante.

Beethoven was furious and this was the reason why I never heard Beethoven play again. He never wanted to play again in my presence and repeatedly demanded that I leave the room when he played. One day when a small party including Beethoven and myself breakfasted with the Prince after the concert in the Augarten (at eight o'clock in the morning), the suggestion was made that we all drive to Beethoven's lodgings to hear his opera, *Leonore*, which had not yet been performed. After we arrived, Beethoven of course demanded that I should leave, and since even the most urgent entreaties of everyone present were to no avail, I did so with tears in my eyes. The whole party noticed it. Prince Lichnowsky followed me and asked that I wait in the anteroom, because since he himself had been the cause of the situation, he now wanted to settle the affair. My injured self-respect, however, would not permit that. I heard afterward that Lichnowsky had become very incensed with Beethoven for his behavior, since only our love for his works had been to blame for the whole incident and consequently also for his anger. These remonstrations, however, only had the effect that he no longer played for that company.

⁂

He composed the third of his string quartets, Opus 18 in D Major, first; the one in F Major, which is now the first, was originally the third.

⁂

Now another anecdote about *Fidelio* or, more correctly, *Leonore*.

Herr Röckel (presently in London) was a tenor at the Wiener Theatre in 1807. The cordiality of his relationship with Beethoven is demonstrated, for example, by the gift of an English dictionary, which is mentioned in a note in my possession. He told me the following anecdote in the spring of 1837. Beethoven's opera, *Leonore*, acknowledged as a failure in 1805, was to be revived in 1807.[58] The main reason for its earlier lack of success was that it premiered just after the French had occupied Vienna. At that time all music lovers and any of the wealthier people who possibly could had fled Vienna, so that there were only French officers in the theater for the most part. Moreover, both the text and the music were extremely drawn out in many places, so that the action proceeded at a very slow pace. Beethoven's friends consequently decided to shorten the opera and called a meeting at Prince Lichnowsky's. This was attended by the Prince, the Princess (who assumed her place at the piano and was known as an excellent pianist), Hofrath von Collin, Stephan von Breuning — these last two had already discussed the cuts to be made — as well as Herr Meyer, the first bass, Herr Röckel, and Beethoven. At the beginning Beethoven defended every measure, but when everyone expressed the opinion that whole numbers would have to be dropped and Herr Meyer claimed that no singer could sing the aria of Pizarro to good effect, Beethoven became rude and angry. Finally he promised to compose a new aria for Pizarro (the present No. 7 in *Fidelio*), and the Prince eventually got him to the point where

Prince Karl (1756-1814) & Princess Maria Lichnowsky (1765-1841)

he conceded that certain things should be left out in the first performance (but only on a trial basis). One could, they maintained, always put them back in again or use them elsewhere. Things couldn't possibly be left to stand as they originally were, since the piece in that condition had failed once already. After long discussion Beethoven gave in — and the cuts were never performed again.

This session lasted from seven o'clock at night until two in the morning, when a cheerful meal brought everything to a pleasant conclusion.

Among the numbers that were cut was a duet in $9/8$ for

two sopranos and, I believe, also an aria and a trio in ¾. The first two numbers are, or were, in the possession of Herr Dunst in Frankfurt. The duet is with violin obligato and was performed here in Frankfurt at the benefit concert for the Beethoven memorial. Easy though it appears, it is difficult and strenuous. Whether more was cut in the revision I do not know.

For this performance Röckel was given the part of Florestan. Florestan's aria, No. 11 (at the beginning of the second act), had concluded with the Adagio in ¾ time in the first version. The Allegro in F major was added later by Beethoven for a tenor who refused to perform otherwise. In the first version Florestan had to sustain the high F at the end for four whole measures of the Adagio, while the orchestra slowly faded away. That particular tenor was incapable of this, and so, presumably in the revision, the part of the Adagio which returns to the key of F major or F minor was left out, and it now passes from A flat major, ¾ Adagio, straight into the Allegro in ¾ time in F major. This version of events was told me by Herr Röckel, who also claims to possess the vocal score in Beethoven's own hand.

⁂

The following note from Beethoven belongs in this context:[59]

Dear Röckel! Do make sure you do a good job with Milder. Just tell her that you are my emissary, sent in advance to beg her not to sing anywhere else. Tomorrow I will come myself to kiss the hem of her gown. Do not forget

Marconi either, and do not get annoyed with me for troubling you with so many things.

Entirely yours,

Beethoven.

*
**

I remember only two occasions where Beethoven instructed me to add a few notes to any of his compositions, once in the Rondo of the *Sonate pathetique* (Opus 13) and another time in the theme of the Rondo in his first Concerto in C Major. There he dictated several octaves to make it more brilliant.

Incidentally, he performed this particular Rondo with a very special expressiveness. In general he played his own compositions most capriciously, though he usually kept a very steady rhythm and only occasionally, indeed, very rarely, speeded up the tempo somewhat. At times he restrained the tempo in his crescendo with a ritardando, which had a beautiful and most striking effect.

In playing he would give various passages, sometimes in the right hand and sometimes in the left, a beautiful, truly inimitable expression, but very rarely indeed did he add notes or embellishments.

*
**

Artistically a most remarkable thing happened with one of his last solo sonatas (in B flat major with the great fugue, Opus 106)[60], which is forty-one pages in print. Beethoven had sent it to me in London to be sold, so that it would be published there at the same time as in Germany. The engraving was finished and I expected daily a letter specifying the day of publication. When the letter arrived, it included the surprising instruction: "Insert at the beginning of the Adagio (which is nine or ten pages long) these two notes as an opening measure."

I must admit that involuntarily I began to wonder if my dear old teacher had really gone daft, a rumor which was going about at the time. To add two notes to such a great work, which had been thoroughly reworked and completed half a year ago!! And yet, I was amazed at the effect of these two notes. Never again could such effective, important notes be added to a completed work, not even if they had been intended from the very beginning. I advise every music lover to try the beginning of this Adagio first without and then with these two notes, which now form the first measure, and there can be no doubt that he will then share my opinion.

Beethoven sent the score of the *Battle of Vittoria* to King George IV of England through the Austrian embassy and dedicated the work to him. He did not hear anything about it for a very long time, except that it had been performed every night at the gala evenings produced by the directors of the Drury Lane Theater, and that it had been greeted with much applause each time. Suddenly I received a letter, sealed in a special envelope and addressed to the King in Beethoven's own hand, enclosed in a letter to me with the instructions to hand it to the King personally. That was impossible, particularly with this king, since only persons of the highest rank, and of these just a select few, were admitted to his presence. Also, the letter itself was rather frightening to look at, since Beethoven had composed it himself and, in his own opinion, had penned it rather beautifully. I turned to Herr von Bauer, the secretary of the Austrian embassy. He answered that the Ambassador could not possibly hand the letter to the King in his position, but that he would try to get it into the King's hands through a private person. This attempt also proved fruitless. Finally I succeeded in arranging the letter's delivery through a page who loved Beethoven's compositions very much. What the letter contained I do not know, but I can state with absolute certainty that no present, not even a word of thanks, ever reached poor Beethoven. He complained greatly about this, and the rebuff probably gave impulse to a droll remark in one of his letters to me: "The King might at least have presented me with a butcher's knife or a turtle." Presumably, Beethoven had heard that the King loved rich and delicate foods, therefore the allusion.

⁂

Beethoven had hardly ever travelled. In his younger years, towards the end of the century, he had once been in Pressburg and Pest and once in Berlin. Even though he showed no difference in his behavior toward people in elevated positions and those of low station, he was not insensitive to the attentions of the former. In Berlin he played at the court (of King Friedrich Wilhelm II) several times, where he also composed and played the two sonatas for cello and piano, Opus 5, for Duport (the King's first cellist) and himself. Upon his departure he received a golden casket filled with Louis d'ors. Beethoven related with pride that it was no ordinary box but one suitable for presentation to ambassadors.

⁂

In Berlin he associated often with Himmel, whose talent he regarded as agreeable, but not much more — his piano playing was elegant and pleasant but not to be compared even with that of Prince Louis Ferdinand. The Prince he had once paid a great compliment, in his opinion, when he observed that he did not play at all like a king or prince, but like a skillful pianist. Himmel and he fell out in the following manner:

Friedrich Heinrich Himmel (1765-1814)

when they were together one day Himmel asked Beethoven to improvise, which Beethoven did. Afterwards Beethoven insisted that Himmel do the same. Himmel was weak enough to agree. After he had played for quite some time, Beethoven said: "Well, when are you actually going to begin?"

Himmel flattered himself that he had been achieving something marvelous already; he therefore left the piano, and both of them exchanged rude remarks with one another.

Beethoven said to me: "I thought Himmel had just been offering a little prelude." They did make up later, but Himmel could only forgive, never forget. They corresponded for some time until Himmel played a mean trick on Beethoven. Beethoven always wanted to hear the latest news from Berlin. This bored Himmel, who finally wrote that the newest thing there was the invention of a lantern for the blind. Beethoven ran about with this piece of news, and of course everyone wanted to know how this was possible. He therefore immediately wrote to Himmel, charging that it was negligent of him not to have sent him any further details.[61]

The answer he received, which cannot be quoted here, not only put an end to their correspondence forever, but brought ridicule on Beethoven, since he was rash enough to show it here and there.

***

When Prince Louis Ferdinand was in Vienna, an old countess held a small musical evening, to which Beethoven was also naturally invited. When the company went in to dinner, the Prince's table was set only for the high nobility — not for Beethoven. He became very agitated, made a few blunt remarks, took his hat and left.

A few days later Prince Louis gave a luncheon, to which some of that party, including the old countess, were invited. When they sat down at the table, the countess was placed on one side of the Prince and Beethoven on the other. He always mentioned this distinction with pleasure.

Archduke Rudolph (1788-1831)

Beethoven was a stranger to rules of etiquette and all that they imply; he never concerned himself about such things. Thus he often acutely embarrassed the entourage of Archduke Rudolph when he first started to frequent that circle. Attempts were made to coerce Beethoven into behaving with the proper deference. This was, however, unbearable for him. He did promise to mend his ways, but that was as far as it went. One day, finally, when he was again, as he termed it, being "sermonized on court manners," he very angrily pushed his way up to the Archduke and said quite frankly that though he had the greatest possible reverence for his person, a strict observance of all the regulations to which his attention was called every day was beyond him. The Archduke laughed good-naturedly about the incident and gave orders to let Beethoven go his own way in peace; he must be taken as he was.

⁂

Beethoven needed a great deal of money, even though he enjoyed very little benefit from it, for he lived very modestly. While he was composing *Leonore*, he had free lodgings in the Wiedner Theater for a year, but since the rooms faced the courtyard, he was not satisfied with them. He therefore rented at the same time lodgings in the Rothes Haus, near the Alster Barracks, where Stephan von Breuning also lived. In the summertime he took rooms in Döbling in the country. As a result of a quarrel with Stephan von Breuning (referred to in Beethoven's letter to me dated 24 July 1804, when Breuning had called in the caretaker as a witness for some statement of his), he commissioned me to find lodgings near the walls of the city. I chose a flat on the Mölker-Bastei in the Pasquillati house; it was on the fourth floor and had a very lovely view. Beethoven then had four apartments at the same time.

He moved out of the last several times but always returned again so that, as I afterwards heard, Baron Pasquillati generously remarked when Beethoven moved out: "The rooms are not to be rented; Beethoven will come back."[62]

⁂

Beethoven attached no importance to his manuscripts.

Once they had been printed, they usually lay about in an adjoining room or scattered on the floor in the middle of his study with other pieces of music. I often put his music in order, but when Beethoven was looking for something, everything was turned upside down again. At any time I could have carried off all those originally autographed compositions that had been engraved already; he would also most likely have given them to me without hesitation had I asked him for them.

⁂

Beethoven had given me his beautiful Concerto in C Minor (Opus 37), still in manuscript, so that I might make my first public appearance as his pupil with it. I am also the only student to make such an appearance during Beethoven's lifetime.

Other than myself he acknowledged only the Archduke Rudolph as his pupil. (Cf. Seyfried, op. cit., p. 12.)[63] Beethoven himself conducted, though he only turned the pages, and it may well be that no concerto was ever accompanied more beautifully.[64] We held two major rehearsals. I had asked Beethoven to compose a cadenza for me, which he refused, and instructing me to write one myself, said he would correct it. Beethoven was very satisfied with my composition and made few changes; but there was an extremely brilliant and very difficult passage in it which, though he liked it, seemed too daring to him. He therefore instructed me to compose another in its place. A week before the performance, he wanted to hear the cadenza again. I played it and bungled the passage; again, somewhat irritated, he told me to change it. I did, but the new one did not satisfy me; I therefore diligently practiced the first one as well, without ever becoming absolutely confident of it. At the concert Beethoven sat down quietly when we reached the cadenza. I could not bring myself to choose the easier one. When I boldly began the more difficult one, Beethoven started violently in his chair. Nevertheless, it came off perfectly, and Beethoven was so pleased that he cried "Bravo!" aloud. This electrified the whole audience and immediately assured my standing among the artists. Later, while expressing his satisfaction with my performance, he added: "But you are stubborn all the same! If you had missed that passage, I would never have given you another lesson again."

⁂

One day Beethoven visited me, carrying his fourth Concerto in G major (Opus 58)[65] tucked under his arm, and said: "Next Saturday you have to play this in the Kärnther-Thor Theater."[65a] Only five days remained to practice it. Unluckily I remarked to him that the time was too short to learn to play it well; would he not permit me to perform the C minor Concerto. Beethoven was annoyed about this, turned on his heels, and went to young Stein, whom he did not really like much. Stein was also a pianist, and in fact had played longer than I. He was clever enough to accept the suggestion immediately. Since he could not finish learning the Concerto either, he went to Beethoven the day before the performance and asked, as I had, if he could play the other one, in C minor. Beethoven more or less had to give in and agreed to this.

However, whether the fault lay with the theater, with the orchestra, or with the pianist himself, the performance was not successful. Beethoven was most annoyed, especially since he was asked by several people: "Why didn't you let Ries play it, since he had such a success with it?" These remarks gave me a great deal of pleasure. Later Beethoven said to me: "I thought you just did not particularly care to play the G major Concerto."

The piano part of the C minor Concerto was never completely written out in the score. Beethoven wrote it down on separate sheets of paper expressly for me.

⁂

In his letter of introduction to Beethoven my father opened a small account for me with him in case I should need it. I never had to make use of it; however, when on several occasions Beethoven noticed I was short of money, he sent me some of his own accord and would never accept repayment. He was really fond of me and once gave me very amusing proof of this affection, in his absent-minded way. I had just returned from Silesia after serving for a rather long period on Beethoven's recommendation as a pianist on the estates of Prince Lichnowsky. I entered the room as he was just about to shave and was covered with soap up to the eyes (his frightfully strong beard grew that high). He jumped up, embraced me cordially, and behold! he had transferred every last bit of lather from his left cheek onto my right.* How we laughed! Beethoven must also have heard privately some stories concerning me, because he knew several of my youthful indiscretions, about which, however, he only teased me. He behaved in a truly paternal fashion toward me on many occasions, including when he was displeased. Once, in 1802, he wrote to me, quite annoyed, about an awkward situation Carl Beethoven had gotten me entangled in: "Don't bother coming to Heiligenstadt, since I have no time to waste." Count Browne was at that time leading a rather high life, and since he took great pleasure in my company, I too often went carousing and neglected my studies in the process.

⁂

Beethoven very much enjoyed looking at women; lovely, youthful faces particularly pleased him. If we passed a girl who could boast her share of charms, he would turn around, look at her sharply again through his glass, then laugh or grin when he realized I was watching him. He was very frequently in love, but usually only for a short time. When once I teased him about his conquest of a certain beautiful lady, he

* *Nil novi sub sole.* "When he (Lord Lovat) was brought to London, Hogarth visited him, finding him in the hands of a barber. Lord Lovat's happiness at seeing his old friend was extraordinary; he jumped up, embraced Hogarth, and conferred upon him, of course, a large portion of the lather on his face." Lichtenberg's *Erklarung*, etc. ninth edition, p. 155.

Wglr.

confessed that she had captivated him more intensely and longer than any other — seven whole months.

One evening I went to Baden to continue my lessons with him. There I found a handsome young woman sitting beside him on the sofa. Feeling that I had come at an inopportune moment, I wanted to leave immediately, but Beethoven detained me and said: "Sit down and play for a while!"

He and the lady remained seated behind me. I had already been playing for a long time when Beethoven suddenly called out: "Ries! Play something romantic!" Soon after: "Something melancholy!" Then: "Something passionate!" and so on.

From what I could hear I deduced that he had evidently offended the lady somehow and now was trying to make up for it by amusing her. Finally he jumped up and shouted: "Why, those are all things I have written!" I had been playing nothing but movements from his own works all the time, connecting them with small transition passages, which seemed to please him. The lady soon left and, to my great surprise, Beethoven did not know who she was. I learned that shortly before I arrived, she had come to the house, wishing to meet Beethoven. We immediately followed her to find out her lodgings and through them later her social position. We could still see her from a distance (it was a moonlit night), but suddenly she disappeared. We then walked another hour and a half or more in the lovely neighboring valley, talking about all kinds of things. In parting, however, Beethoven said: "I must find out who she is and you must help me." A long time afterward I met her in Vienna and discovered that she was the mistress of a foreign prince. I told Beethoven the news but never heard anything more about her, neither from him nor from anyone else.

Beethoven never visited me more frequently than when I lived in a house owned by a tailor with three very beautiful but absolutely irreproachable daughters. He refers to them at the conclusion of his letter of 24 July 1804 when he says: "Do not do too much tailoring, remember me to the fairest of the fair, send me half a dozen sewing needles!"

⁂

Even after he reached Vienna, Beethoven had taken violin lessons with Krumpholz,[66] and when I was first there, we sometimes played his piano and violin sonatas together.* That was, however, truly dreadful music-making, because in the throes of his enthusiasm he did not hear when he attacked a passage with the wrong fingering.

Beethoven was most awkward and bungling in his behavior; his clumsy movements lacked all grace. He rarely picked up anything without dropping or breaking it. Thus he frequently knocked his inkwell into the piano, which stood beside his writing desk. No piece of furniture was safe from him, least of all anything valuable. Everything was knocked

---

* That is, when his hearing was already impaired!

Wglr.

over, soiled, or destroyed. How he ever managed to shave himself at all remains difficult to understand, even considering the frequent cuts on his cheeks. — He never learned to dance in time with the music.

***

Beethoven's String Quintet (Opus 29) in C Major had been sold to a publisher in Leipzig but was stolen in Vienna and suddenly published by A. & Company.[66a] Since it had been copied in one night, there were innumerable mistakes in it, and even whole bars were missing. Beethoven here behaved in such an exemplary fashion that one would be hard put to find anywhere another example of such manners. He asked A. to send the fifty copies which had already been printed to me at home for correction, while at the same time telling me to make the corrections in ink so roughly on the poor paper and to cross out several lines in such a way that it would be impossible to use a copy or to sell it. Most of the crossing out occurred in the Scherzo. I followed these instructions faithfully, and A. had to melt down the plates to avoid a law suit.

***

Beethoven was very forgetful in many things. Once he had received a handsome riding horse as a present from Count Browne in return for the dedication of the Variations in A Major, No. 5 on a Russian Song.[67] He rode it a few times but soon forgot all about it and, what was worse, forgot all about feeding it too. His servant soon noticed this and started hiring out the horse to his own advantage. So as not to attract Beethoven's attention, he put off handing him a bill for the fodder for a very long time. At last, however, to Beethoven's great astonishment, a rather large feed bill was presented to him, which suddenly recalled to him the existence of his horse, as well as his negligence in regard to it.

⁂

During the short bombardment of Vienna by the French in 1809, Beethoven was very frightened. He spent most of the time in the cellar at his brother Caspar's house, where he covered his head with pillows to shut out the sound of the cannons.*

⁂

Beethoven was at times extremely short-tempered. One day we were eating lunch in the Swan Inn, and the waiter brought him the wrong dish. No sooner had Beethoven remarked about it — and received an answer from the waiter which was not exactly deferential — then he took the dish (it was a so-called Lungenbratel, a roast with plenty of gravy) and flung it at the waiter's head. The poor man carried a large number of plates piled with food on his arm (the Viennese

---

* Might not the thundering of the cannons have been painful for his suffering ears?

Wglr.

waiters are extremely clever at that), so he was quite helpless. The gravy ran down his face. He and Beethoven shouted and abused each other, while all the other guests laughed loudly. Finally, Beethoven broke off and burst out laughing also at the sight of the waiter with gravy dripping down his face, licking it up with his tongue, trying to curse but forced to resume licking up the gravy and pulling the most ludicrous faces. A picture worthy of a Hogarth.

***

Beethoven had hardly any understanding of money, which often gave rise to the most unpleasant scenes. Suspicious by nature, he often thought himself cheated when this was not the case. Easily excited, he would call people cheats to their faces and, where waiters were concerned, often had to make up for it with a tip. Finally his peculiarities and absent-mindedness became known in the inns he most frequently visited, and anything was tolerated, even if he left without paying.

***

Beethoven remembered his early youth and his friends from Bonn with much pleasure, although in reality those had been difficult times for him. Of his mother especially he spoke with love and affection, and often called her a fine, truly kindhearted woman. He did not like talking about his father, who was mainly at fault for the family misfortunes, but any harsh word about him let fall by a third person made

Beethoven angry. In general he was a thoroughly kind person at heart, only his temper and irritability often got him into trouble. And no matter what insult or injustice had been done him by anyone, Beethoven would have forgiven him on the spot, had he met him when crushed by misfortune.

Johann van Beethoven (1740-1792), the Composer's Father

Beethoven's way of conducting business was rather peculiar. For instance, he had commissioned me to sell his piano sonatas (Opus 110 and 111) and 33 Variations on a Waltz (Opus 120), which he expected to send to me soon in London. I had already come to an agreement with Messrs. Clementi & Company for the sonatas and with Boosey, the music publishers, concerning a fee for the Variations, and I was waiting for the works to arrive. Finally they came. To my surprise I saw that in very large, even letters drawn by his own hand on the title page, Beethoven had dedicated the Variations to my wife.[67a] This dedication, however, is found only on that single copy which is still in my possession.

Beethoven had put off sending these manuscripts for so long that in the meantime he had completely forgotten what he had instructed me to do. When I took the Variations to Boosey, we discovered not only that they were the same as a set already published in Vienna — with a dedication to Madame Brentano — but also one sonata had already been printed in Paris!

⁂

Beethoven had enclosed a few insignificant pieces (the second collection of Bagatelles), some of which had better not been published at all; I sold them immediately for twenty-five guineas, wrote Beethoven how everything worked out, and received a response charging me with negligence. He apologized for the double dedication. To my amazement he pointedly mentioned: "I would never think of accepting a present or a gratuity for it!" One could hardly find a more sudden about-face or a more obvious self-contradiction!

⁂

I have grave doubts about manuscripts found in Beethoven's estate. I shall only recognize *oeuvres posthumes* as genuine after I have seen a copy in his own handwriting or otherwise properly verified.

My reasons are as follows:

First: when I was with him from 1800 to November, 1805, and later in 1809, when I returned to Vienna, there were no manuscripts on hand because Beethoven was always behind with commissioned compositions right up to the day of his death.

Secondly: all his little compositions and many things he never wanted published, since he did not consider them worthy of his name, were secretly brought out by his brothers. Thus songs he had composed in Bonn years before his departure for Vienna became known only after he had achieved a high reputation. Even small compositions which he had written in autograph albums were purloined and engraved in this way.

Thirdly: as almost all the letters I received from him in England dealt with money difficulties, why wouldn't he have sent me the manuscripts straightaway, had he had any?

Once, after a lot of effort, I had prevailed upon the Philharmonic Society in London to order three overtures from him, which were to remain the Society's property. He sent me three, none of which we could perform in view of Beethoven's great reputation, since at these concerts everyone eagerly looked forward to, indeed demanded, something out of the ordinary from him. He had all three published a few years later, but the Society did not find it worth its while to complain. Among them was the *Overture to the Ruins of Athens*, which I consider unworthy of him.

If Beethoven had had anything better in manuscript, he would certainly have sent it to this Society; that is quite clear from all his letters. Since he also frequently claimed he could live by his pen alone, I find it virtually impossible to acknowledge as authentic the three piano quartets published by

Artaria after his death.

Beethoven could not have patched together from old themes a gigantic work like the three sonatas (Opus 2), dedicated to Haydn, which immediately created such a sensation throughout the world. Nor would he have employed these themes years later in empty, badly written quartets. After all, his mind kept pouring forth new ideas incessantly until his death.

Without wanting to hurt the feelings of any composers living or dead, I must reaffirm my belief that no one else showed such a wealth and variety of ideas, nor such originality, as Beethoven did in his works. Even though Beethoven as a friend and teacher stood and remains above all others for me, I have never been known as the sort who reveres only one or at the most two musical idols and judges everything not by them as mediocre, if not downright bad, in advance. Such one-sidedness never will be a failing of mine.

⁂

Now follow several letters of Beethoven's, all of them written entirely in his own hand except one, which is but partially in autograph. Most of them offer corroboration of what I have written above, providing more details or elaborating on what I have said.

A small portion of the following consists of notes, usually without specific dates, through which he gave instructions to me as his pupil. Then come more recent letters up to the year 1825. During my travels through North

Germany, Russia, Sweden, and Denmark I very rarely heard from him directly, but after I settled in England, he wrote quite often. Everything else should be clear from the letters themselves.

Some of Beethoven's letters containing very definite and most uncomplimentary opinions about certain people I have withheld, at least for the time being, if not, I hope, forever. Why should anyone either through harassment or negotiation put pressure on me to do otherwise?*

***

(Undated, no address)

(Vienna, probably 1801)

Here, dear Ries! Take these four parts which I have corrected and check the other copies against them right away. . . . Here is the letter to Count Browne; it says that he must give you the 50# (ducats) in advance because you have to buy some things for yourself. He cannot take offense at that since as soon as you have finished, you will be leaving for Baden with him next Monday. All the same, I must reproach you for not having turned to me much sooner. Do you not consider me your true friend? Why do you hide your need from me? None of my friends should go in want as long as I have anything; I would have

---

* I, too, possibly even more sensitive about this since the death of my friend than he was during his own life, would like to add a warning to this effect, since I am fully familiar with the subject as well as the content of the letters in question.

Wglr.

already sent you a small sum if I were not relying on Browne to help you; if that fails, turn immediately to your friend.

Beethoven

***

(1803)

You probably already know that I am here. Go to Stein and find out whether he cannot deliver an instrument to me — to be paid for. I am worried about having mine carted out here. Come this evening around seven o'clock. My lodgings are in Oberdöbling No. 4(1)*, on the left side of the road where one goes down the hill to Heiligenstadt.*

(1) A village near Vienna.

***

(Probably 1804)

Dear Ries! Please do have the kindness to copy this Andante(1)*, even if only poorly. I must send it off tomorrow and — since heaven alone knows what might happen to it — I would like to have a copy. But I must have it back around one o'clock tomorrow. The reason why I am bothering you with this chore is that one copyist is occupied with other important things and the other is ill.*

(1) It was, unless my memory fails me, the Grand Andante with Variations from the Kreuzer Sonata for piano and violin, Opus 47.[68]

***

Baden, 14 July 1804

If you, dear Ries, could manage to find me better lodgings, I would really appreciate it. — I would very much like to have rooms on a large, quiet square or on the ramparts. — I will make every effort to be at the rehearsal on Wednesday. I am not pleased that it is at Schuppanzigh's. He ought to be grateful if all my insults have caused him to lose a little weight.*[68a] *Stay well, dear Ries! We are having bad weather, and I am not safe from people here. I must run away to be alone.*

***

(Vienna, probably the beginning of July, 1804)

Dear Ries, Since Breuning did not hesitate in his behavior to represent my character to you and to the caretaker in such a light that I appear as a miserable, wretched, mean man, I choose you to convey my answer to Breuning directly. But tell him I am replying to only one point, indeed the first point, of his letter, which I do only to justify my character to you! — Tell him, therefore, that I had not considered reproaching him for the delay in giving notice and that, if it was really Breuning's fault, any harmonious relationship in this world is far too valuable and dear to me to hurt one of my friends for the sake of a few hundred or even more. You yourself know that I had accused you in jest that it was your fault that the notice had come too late. I know for sure you will remember that; I had forgotten the whole affair. Then my brother started up again, while we were sitting at the table, and said that he thought Breuning was at fault there. I denied it on the spot and said that it was your fault. Surely it was clear enough that I did not blame Breuning. Breuning, however, jumped up in a frenzy and said that he wanted to call in the

---

* A verification of my opinion in Note 6 to the letter of 2 November 1793. Wglr.

caretaker. I was not used to such behavior from any of the the people with whom I am friends, and it made me lose my self-control. I also jumped up, knocked my chair over, went away and did not come back. This behavior then induced Breuning to present me in such a nice light in front of you and the caretaker. He also wrote me a letter, which, incidentally, I have answered only with silence. — I have nothing more to say to Breuning. His way of thinking and acting toward me proves that no friendly relationship should ever have existed between us and certainly shall not exist in future. I wanted to acquaint you with this, because you have misunderstood and belittled everything I said and did in this instance. I know that, had you known the affair as it really was, you certainly would not have done so and am satisfied with that.(1)

Now I ask you, dear Ries, immediately upon receipt of this letter to visit my brother the pharmacist and tell him that I shall be leaving Baden in a few days and that he should rent the lodgings for me in Döbling immediately now that you have notified him. I almost came today; I loathe it here and am tired of it all. For heaven's sake urge him to rent it immediately, for I want to stay there straight away. Don't tell Breuning anything, and show him nothing of the letter written on the other side. I want to demonstrate in every way possible that I am not as small-minded as he and that I have written him only after sending this letter to you, even though the decision to sever our friendship is and remains fast.

Your friend,

Beethoven.

(1) The real basis for the quarrel mentioned in this letter is probably connected with an eviction notice on one of Beethoven's lodgings postponed or ignored by Breuning (because at that time Beethoven lived in the Theater auf der Wieden). Breuning, a hothead like Beethoven, was especially

enraged about his friend's behavior, as Beethoven himself describes it here, because it happened in the presence of Beethoven's brother. — The following letter is a sequel to this. A few months later the two met by accident, and a complete reconciliation took place. Beethoven's hostile intentions, however vehemently proclaimed in the two letters, were completely forgotten. Beethoven's letters prove this at several points, as do those written by Breuning. Beethoven dedicated a work (Opus 61) to him and named him as joint guardian of his nephew. Incidentally, the two letters with their sequels, particularly the next letter, are too fine a documentation of Beethoven's character not to be included here.

⁂

Baden, 24 July 1804

. . .You will surely have been surprised over the affair with Breuning. Do believe me, my dear friend, when I say that my explosion was only the culmination of several previous unpleasant incidents with him. I have the gift of concealing and containing my sensitivity to a great many things. But if I am ever irritated at a time when I am more susceptible to aggravation, then I lose my temper more violently than any other man. Breuning certainly has some excellent qualities, but he thinks himself free of all fault, and usually suffers to the greatest degree from precisely those weaknesses he divines in other people. He has a meanness of spirit which I have despised since childhood. My good sense had almost discerned the way things would go with Breuning, since our way of thinking, acting, and feeling differs too much, but I had thought that these difficulties might also be overcome. — Experience has proved me wrong. And now I have had enough of friendship! I have found only two friends in this

world with whom things have not gone sour at some point. And what men! One is dead; the other is still living.[69] *Even though for almost six years now neither of us has heard anything of the other, nevertheless, I know I occupy the first place in his heart, as he does in mine. True friendship must be grounded in the rarest similarity of heart and soul in men. I wish only that you should read the letter which I wrote to Breuning and his letter to me. No, never again will he command the place in my heart that he once had. Anyone who can attribute to his friends such a low level of thinking and could respond himself by behaving in such a manner — he is not worth my friendship. — Don't forget to see to my lodgings. Stay well. Don't do too much tailoring, remember me to the fairest of the fair, and send me half a dozen sewing needles. — I would never in my life have believed that I could be so lazy as I am here. If I should suddenly be seized with energy, something worthwhile might possibly result.*

Vale.

Beethoven

⁂

(Undated. Written a few days before the French invasion, 1805)

Please excuse me, your serene highness, if the bearer of this message should alarm you. Poor Ries, my pupil, is being forced to take up arms in this miserable war[(1)]*, and is, furthermore, obliged to depart from us in a few days because he is an alien. — He has nothing to his name, absolutely nothing, and must make a long journey. The opportunity to appear at an Academy concert is now entirely lost to him because of these circumstances. He must take refuge in charity. I recommend him to you. I know you will excuse my boldness. Only extreme need could force a high-minded man to plead in such a way for another's generosity.*

With complete confidence I send the poor fellow to you, hoping you will lighten somewhat the burden of his difficulties. He must appeal to everyone who knows him.

With deepest respect,
L. van Beethoven(2)

(Address) *Pour Madame la Princesse Liechtenstein*, etc.

(1) Being born on the left bank of the Rhine, I was conscripted under a French law.

(2) The letter was never delivered (to Beethoven's great anger), but I preserved the original written on a small, unevenly cut quarter sheet as a testimony of Beethoven's friendship and love for me.

***

(1809)

Your friends, my dear fellow, have certainly given you some bad advice. But I know them — they are the same people from whom you gathered the pleasant news you sent me from Paris(1)*, who inquired after my age, which you were so good as to supply,*(2) *who have lowered you in my estimation several times already and now forever.*

Farewell,(3)

Beethoven.

(1) I no longer recollect the immediate reason for this note. I had written from Paris that musical taste there was poor and few of Beethoven's works were known or performed there.

(2) Some friends of Beethoven wanted to know his birthday for certain. I spent a great deal of effort looking for his baptismal certificate when I was in Bonn in 1806. Finally I

found it and sent it to Vienna. He never liked to speak of his age.

(3) He soon got over his irritation, and the former friendship was resumed.

***

Wednesday, 22 November. Vienna, 1815

Dear Ries, I write in haste to tell you that I have sent the piano score of the Symphony in A to Messrs. Thomas Coutts & Co. by post today. Since the Court is not here, couriers are rare or nonexistent, and in any case this is the safest way. The symphony should come out about March; I will determine the day. It took too long this time for me to set a more specific deadline. — The trio in the violin sonata may take longer; both will be in London within a few weeks. — I urgently entreat you, dear Ries, to take an interest in this matter yourself to be sure that I receive the money. It costs so much before everything is finished and I need it.

I have suffered a reduction of 600 florin annually in my salary; at the time of the B.N. (bank notes) it was nothing at all. — Then came the redemption (certificates), and because of them I lost these 600 florin. After several years of aggravation and virtual disappearance of the stipend we have now reached the point where the R.C. (redemption certificates) are worse than the B.N. (bank notes) ever were. I pay 1,000 florins rent. Imagine the misery this paper money causes. My poor unfortunate brother (Carl) has just died; he had a wretched wife; I might add that he had consumption for several years, and what money I gave to make life easier for him I figure must come to some 10,000 florin V.C. (Viennese currency). This is of course nothing to an Englishman, but, for a poor German — or worse yet, an Austrian — it amounts to a great deal. The poor man changed terribly in his last years, and I must say I pitied him with my whole heart. Now I am very happy to be able to say that as far as his support was concerned I have no need to reproach myself. — Tell Mr. Birchall that he should recompense Mr. Salomon[70] *and yourself for the postal expenses incurred by your letters to me and mine to you; he can deduct it from the sum due me; I want those who act on my behalf to suffer as little as possible.*

Wellington's Victory in the Battle of Vittoria(1) *must long since have arrived at Th. Coutts & Co. Mr. Birchall need not pay the fee until he has received all the compositions. Do hurry and let me know the date when Mr. Birchall can bring out the piano reduction. Other than that I urge you heartily to keep looking after my affairs generally; I am at your service however you might need me. With my most cordial wishes, dear Ries!*

Your friend

Beethoven

(1) This is the same as the title on the piano reduction. (Beethoven's own note.)

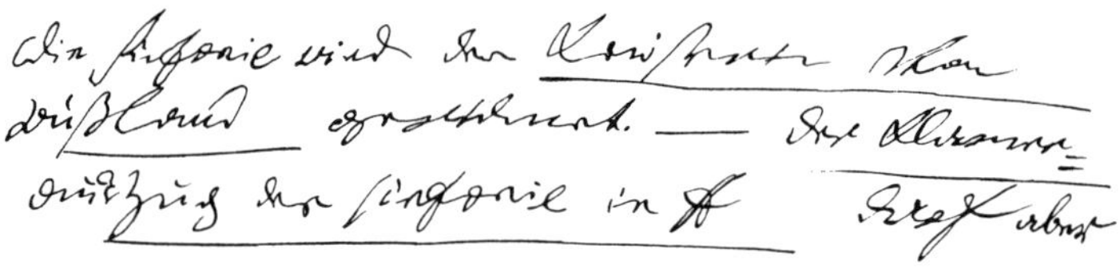

Excerpt from Beethoven's letter to Ferdinand Ries, 20 January 1816

⁂

Vienna, 20 January 1816

My dear Ries, The Symphony is dedicated to the Empress of Russia. The piano score of the Symphony in A must not be published before the month of June; the publisher here cannot manage it earlier. Convey this immediately to Mr. Birchall, dear, kind Ries. — The sonata with violin, which will be sent by next post, can also be published in London in the month of May. The trio, however, later.[71] *(It will also arrive with the next post.) I will set the date for it later.*

And now, my heartfelt thanks, dear Ries, for all the kindness you show me, and particularly for the corrections. May heaven bless you and may you enjoy ever greater success, in which I take the most cordial interest. My greetings to your wife!

As always. Your true friend

Ludwig van Beethoven.

***

28 February 1816

. . .I have not been well for some time; my brother's death affected my spirits and my work.

Salomon's death grieves me greatly because he was a noble man whom I remember even from my childhood. You have become the executor of his will, and I at the same time guardian of my poor late brother's child. You will hardly have had as much aggravation as I have had over that death; yet I have the sweet consolation of having saved a poor innocent child from the hands of an unworthy mother.

Fare well, my dear Ries! If I can serve you in any way, do consider me only as your very true friend

Beethoven.

***

Vienna, 8 March 1816

My answer comes somewhat late. — However, I was ill and have had a lot to do. . . . Not a penny of the 10 ducats in gold has arrived so far, and I am beginning to believe that the English, too, are only generous when abroad; the same applies to the Prince Regent, from whom I did not even receive the copying costs for my Battle *which I sent him, indeed not even a word or note of thanks. . . . My salary amounts to 3400 florins in paper money. I pay 1100 rent; my servant and his wife 900 fl.; you can work out what remains. At the same time I have to support my little nephew completely; until now he has been*

Karl van Beethoven, Beethoven's nephew (1806-1858)

at boarding school; this costs up to 1100 fl. and is still not satisfactory, so that I have to establish a regular household before I can bring him to live with me. How much one has to earn merely to be able to live here; and yet there is no end to it, because — because — because — you know what I mean.

A few commissions from the Philharmonic Society, apart from an Academy concert, would also be highly welcome.

Incidentally, my dear pupil Ries ought to sit down and dedicate something good to me, whereupon the Master would respond by repaying him in kind.[(1)] *How shall I send you my portrait? . . . My best wishes to your wife; alas, I have none; I found only one, whom I will most likely never possess,*[72] *but that does not make me a woman hater.*[(2)]

Your true friend
Beethoven

(1) Cf. Note 1 to Beethoven's letter of 2 May 1810.

(2) Cf. Note 4 to Beethoven's letter of 16 November 1801.

***

Vienna, 3 April 1816

. . .Neate must presumably be in London now; I have given him several compositions of mine and he promised to put them to good use, to my advantage. . .Archduke Rudolph also plays your works with me, my dear Ries! of which il sogno *has pleased me particularly well. Fare well, salutations to your dear wife, and to all the beautiful English ladies whom it might please — my personal greetings.*

Your true friend

Beethoven.

***

Vienna, 11 June 1816[73]

My dear Ries,

I am sorry that you have to spend postage money again for my sake; though I may be happy to help and serve all men, it hurts me to have to take advantage of others. Of the 10 ducats still nothing has appeared,[74] *and so one must come to the conclusion that in England, as here, there are windbags and people who do not keep their word. — I do not blame you for this at all.*[75]*. . .Since I also have not heard a single syllable from Neate,*[76] *I would ask you simply to inquire*[77] *whether he has succeeded in selling the Concerto*[78] *in F Minor.*[79] *I am almost ashamed to speak of all the other works which I gave him. I mean ashamed of myself*[80] *for handing them over to him so trustingly,*[81] *so completely without any conditions other than those which I invented in the name of friendship and conscience.*[82]

Someone gave me a translation of a notice in the Morning Chronicle[83] *about the performance of the Symphony (probably the one in A).*[84] *Undoubtedly this and all the other works taken along by Neate*[85] *will turn out like the* Battle (of Vittoria)[86]*, that is, I'll most likely enjoy no benefit from them*[87] *other than reading about performances in the newspapers.*[88, 89]

***

Vienna, 9 July 1817

Dear friend,

The offers made in your kind letter of 9 June are most flattering. This letter is meant to show you how much I appreciate them. Were it not for my unfortunate handicap, which entails considerable care and expense, especially while traveling and in a foreign country, I would unquestionably accept the proposal of the Philharmonic Society.

Put yourself, however, in my position. Consider how many more obstacles I must fight than any other artist, and then judge whether my demands are excessive. Here they are, and I would ask you to convey them to the directors of this particular Society.

1) I will be in London by the first half of the month of January, 1818, at the latest.

2) The two grand symphonies, entirely new, shall be ready then, and they will be and will remain the whole property of the Society.

3) The Society is to give me 300 guineas for them, plus 100 guineas toward traveling expenses, which will, however, come to much more, as I absolutely must take a companion with me.

4) Since I shall commence work on the composition of these grand symphonies immediately, the Society shall (upon acceptance of my conditions) transmit the sum of 150 guineas to me here, so that I can equip myself with a carriage and other necessities for the journey without delay.

5) The condition that I not appear with another orchestra in public, that I not conduct, and that the Society have precedence in other, similar instances, I accept. These restrictions could have gone without saying, from my sense of honor alone.

6) I may rely on the Society's assistance in preparing and promoting one or more benefit concerts for myself, depending on circumstances. Both the special friendship of several directors of your honorable Reunion, *as well as the musician's kind interest in my works, vouches for such cooperation and encourages me all the more to fulfill the general expectations.*

7) I further ask to receive the agreement or confirmation of the above in the English language, signed by three directors in the name of the Society.

You can well imagine how much I look forward to meeting the worthy Sir George Smart and to seeing you and Mr. Neate again. If only I could fly there myself in place of this letter!

Your loyal admirer and friend

L. v. Beethoven

(P.S. in Beethoven's own hand)

Dear Ries, I embrace you warmly; I intentionally engaged another hand for the above so that you could read all of it better and present it to the Society. I am convinced of your good will toward me and hope that the Philharmonic Society will agree to my proposal. You need have no doubt that I will do everything within my power to fulfill properly the commission with which such a select society of artists has greatly honored me. — How large is your orchestra? How many violins, etc., etc.? Single or double winds? Is the hall large, resonant?

***

Vienna, 5 March 1818

My dear Ries,

Much though I wished to, I could not come to London this year; please inform the Philharmonic Society that weak health prevented me. I do hope, however, to be fully recovered this spring. Then later in the year I will be able to respond to the Society's offer and shall fulfill all the conditions thereof. Tell Neate I wish he would not play, in public at least, any of the various works which he took from me until I come. However things may have worked out with him, I have reason to complain about his behavior.

Botter[90] *visited me a few times; he seems to be a good man and has a talent for composition. — I hope and pray that your fortune improves daily. Alas, I cannot say the same about myself. . . . I can never see anyone in need but what I must give him something. Therefore you can well imagine that this whole business is even more insufferable. Please do write me soon. If at all possible, I shall leave here even earlier to avoid being utterly ruined, and then I shall arrive in London during this winter at the latest. I know you will stand by your unhappy friend. If only it had been within my power and I had not been fettered by circumstances here as always, I would certainly have done far more for you. — Farewell; give my regards to Neate, Smart, Cramer — even though I hear that he is a creature at odds with you and me. In the meantime I have learned the art of dealing with things like that a little better, and in London we will produce a pleasant harmony in spite of everything.*

I greet and embrace you with all my heart.

Your friend

Ludwig van Beethoven.

My cordial greetings to your dear, beautiful (so I hear) wife.

***

Vienna, 30 April 1819

My dear Ries,

Only now can I answer your last letter of 18 December. Your sympathy comforts me. For the moment it is impossible to come to London, entangled as I am in various difficulties. But God will speed me to London next winter surely; then I will also bring the new symphonies. I am expecting the text for a new oratorio I am writing for the Musik-Verein *here, which ought to serve us in London too. Do for me what you can, because I need the help. Commissions from the Philharmonic Society would have been very welcome to me. The reports which Neate has sent me in the meanwhile about the virtual failure of the three overtures have upset me; each one was, in its own way, not only well received here, but those in E Flat and C Major even made a great impression.*[91] *The fate of these compositions with the Philharmonic Society is incomprehensible to me. You will by now have received the Quintet arrangement*[92] *and the Sonata. Make sure that both works, but especially the Quintet, are printed immediately. It may take a little longer with the Sonata, but I would wish for it to appear at least within two or, at the most, three months. The earlier letter you mention I did not receive. Therefore I did not hesitate to hawk the two works here as well — but for the rights in Germany only. Meanwhile, it will be another three months before the Sonata is published here;*[93] *just hurry with the Quintet. As soon as you send me the money, I will send a statement certifying the publisher as owner of these works for England, Scotland, Ireland, France, etc.*

You will receive the tempi *according to Mälzel's metronome with the next post. De Smidt, Prince Paul Esterhazy's courier, has taken the Quintet and the Sonata with him. At the earliest opportunity you will also receive my portrait, since I hear you really want one.*

Farewell. Remain fond of me, your friend

Beethoven

Beautiful greetings to your beautiful wife!!!

From me!!!!!

Vienna, 16 April 1819

Herewith, dear Ries, the tempi for the Sonata.

1st Allegro, but only Allegro, the *assai* must go.

Mälzel's metronome 𝅗𝅥 = 138.

2nd piece scherzoso.[94] *M. metronome* 𝅗𝅥 = *80.*

3rd piece M. metronome ♪ = *92.*

Note here that the first bar still must be inserted as follows:

1st bar

4th piece Introduzione largo. *Mälzel's metronome* 𝅘𝅥𝅯 = *76.*

5th piece, 3/4 time.

and the last, Mälzel's metronome 𝅗𝅥 = *144.*

Forgive the confusion; if you knew my situation, you would not be surprised. You would instead be amazed at what I can still achieve. The Quintet finally cannot be delayed any longer and will appear very soon. The Sonata, however, must not appear, until I finally receive your answer and the payment I yearn for. De Smit is the name of the courier through whom you received the Quintet as well as the Sonata. — I beg you for an early answer. More next time! Hurriedly

Your

Beethoven

⁂

19 April 1819

Dear friend,

Please do forgive me the inconvenience I am causing you. It is incomprehensible to me how so many mistakes could creep into the copy of the Sonata — the incorrect copying probably stems from the fact that I can no longer keep my own copyist. Circumstances have brought that about, and may God preserve me until . . . finds himself in a better position! This may take yet another full year. — It is truly dreadful how this business has transpired and what has become of my salary. No one can say what will happen until the year is over. Should the Sonata (Opus 106) not be suitable for London, I could send another one; or you might also leave out the Largo *and start straightaway with the fugue in the last section; or use the first section, then the Adagio, and for the third movement the* Scherzo *and the Largo and* A^llo.^ risoluto. *— I leave all that to you; do as you think best.*[(1)] *. . . The Sonata was written under oppressive circumstances. It is hard to write almost for the sake of bread alone, and it has now come to that.*

Let us keep in touch about my coming to London. It would certainly be the only way to extricate myself from this miserable anxiety-producing situation. Here I shall never regain my health nor achieve what I might under better circumstances.

(1) What a wealth of suggestions! What range! Was this because he foresaw the difficulty of selling it?

⁂

Vienna, 25 May 1819

. . . *In the meantime I have been burdened with more worries than ever before in my life, all as a result of excessive generosity to other people.*

Compose diligently! My dear little Archduke Rudolf and I play your things too, and he says that the former pupil is a credit to the master. — Farewell for now. Since I hear that your wife is beautiful, here is a kiss for her — in thought only, though I hope to have that pleasure next winter. — Do not forget the Quintet and the Sonata and the money, I might say the honorarium, avec ou sans honneur.

I hope to hear the very best from you, not in allegro fashion but Veloce Prestissimo. *The bearer of this letter is a clever Englishman. Most of his countrymen are bright fellows with whom I would like to spend some time in their own country.*

Prestissimo — Responsio, il suo amico e Maestro

Beethoven

⁂

Vienna, 10 November 1819

Dear Ries,

I am writing to tell you that the Sonata has already been published. But only about fourteen days ago. Because it is almost six months since both works — the Quintet and the Sonata — were sent to you. I will send you engraved copies of both the Quintet and Sonata by courier within a few days. Then you can correct everything in both works.

Since I did not receive a letter from you about the receipt of the two works, I thought nothing was coming of it. — After all, I have already been shipwrecked once this year, thanks to Neate. I wish now that you would just find some way to obtain the 50 ducats, since I was counting on them and really need a lot of money. I've written enough for today. I'd just like to add that I have nearly completed a new grand mass. Let me know what you could do with it in L. (London). But soon, very soon, and send the money for the two works soon as well. — Next time I will write you in more detail. In haste! Your good true friend

Beethoven

⁂

Vienna, 6 April 1822

Dear, most excellent Ries,

Again for over half a year now I have not been well and could never answer your letter. I received the 26 pounds sterling in good order, and thank you cordially for it. I have received nothing of your symphony dedicated to me. . . . My greatest work is a grand mass[95] *which I wrote recently, etc., etc. Time is too short today, therefore only the essentials. . . . What would the Philharmonic Society offer me for a symphony?*

I am still thinking of coming to London, if only my health would permit, possibly next spring?! — You would find me truly appreciative of my dear pupil, who has now become a great master. Who knows what other good things in the cause of art might result from our joint efforts? I am, as always, completely devoted to my muses, and in this alone do I find the happiness of my life. I also act and work for others as best I can. . . . You have two children; I have one (my brother's son). But you are married, so your two do not cost you as much as the one costs me.

Now farewell. Kiss your beautiful wife, until I can perform this ceremonial act in person.

Cordially your friend

Beethoven

P.S. Make sure that I receive your dedication, so that I can respond in kind, which I shall do immediately upon receiving it.[96]

***

Vienna, 20 December 1822

My dear Ries!

Since I have been overburdened with work, I am only now able to answer your letter of 15 November — I am delighted to accept the commission to write a new symphony for the Philharmonic Society. Even if the honorarium from the English cannot be compared with fees paid by other nations, I would even compose free of charge for the foremost artists in Europe if I were not still the poor Beethoven. If only I were in London, what wouldn't I write for the Philharmonic Society! Because Beethoven can compose, thank God, though he may not be able to do anything else in this world. If only God would restore my health, which has at least improved, then I could fulfill all the offers from all over Europe, indeed even from North America,[97] *and might yet get my life in order.*

(Excerpt from a letter the beginning of which is missing)

. . . Pursue everything as soon as possible for your poor friend. I also await your plans for my journey.[(1)] *This really has become annoying; it aggravates me more than ever; if it does not work out, it will be just too much! A* crimen laesae*! . . . Apparently you want me to dedicate something to you soon. I shall most gladly comply, more gladly than for any of those great lords,* entre nous. *The devil knows what can happen at their hands. I will dedicate the new symphony to you (the Ninth, with chorus). — I hope I shall finally receive a dedication from you. . . . "B" should open the letter to the King (George IV) which he took with him; he will then see what I wrote his Highness about the* Battle of Vittoria. *The next letter to him (the King)*[(2)] *contains the same, but with no mention of the mass. — Our amiable friend B.*[**97a**] *might see if he cannot at least extract a butcher's knife or a turtle in return. Obviously the engraved score of the* Battle *should also be given to the King. — This letter will cost you a great deal of money*[(3)]*, subtract it from what you are sending me. How sorry I am to inconvenience you!*

God be with you. Cordial greetings to your wife until I am there myself. Watch out! — you believe me old, I am a young old man. As always

Yours

(1) The plan of how Beethoven was to arrange his journey to England.

(2) The letter, affixed with two seals, was in Beethoven's own hand, as was the address on the envelope. It was enclosed in a letter to me, which had been inserted in another envelope. Since the first address to me evidently seemed illegible even to him, he made a third envelope around it without taking off the second.

(3) 17 shillings = 10 ⅕ florin.

Vienna, 25 April 1823

Dear Ries!

The Cardinal's (Archduke Rudolph) sojourn here for four weeks, when I had to give him two and a half or even three hours of lessons each day, robbed me of a great deal of time. After such lessons one is hardly able to think the next day, much less compose. —

My permanently depressing situation, however, demands that I write just now whatever brings me enough money for my immediate needs. What sad disclosures you are hearing!! Now, because of the many troubles I have been enduring, I am not well; even my eyes are sore! However, do not worry. You will receive the symphony shortly; really only this miserable situation is at fault. — Within a few weeks you will also receive 33 new variations on a theme (Waltz, Opus 120), dedicated to your wife.

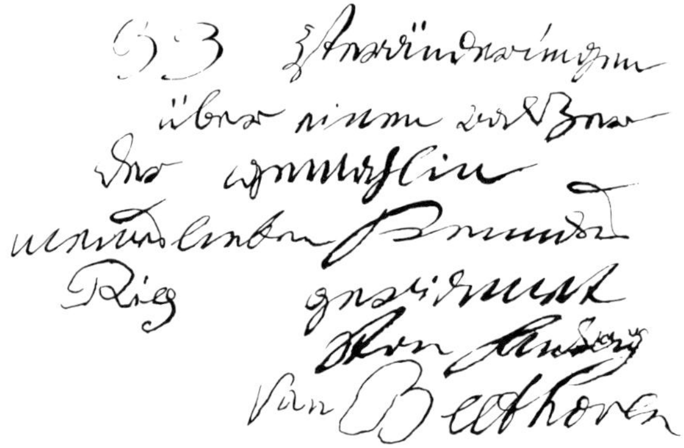

Excerpt from Beethoven's letter to Ferdinand Ries, 25 April 1823

Bauer (First Secretary of the Imperial Embassy) has the score of the Battle of Vittoria, *which . . . was dedicated to the former Prince Regent and for which I am still owed the copying costs . . . I only ask you, dear friend! to send me as soon as possible whatever you can get for it. — After all, we both know those gentlemen, the publishers . . . As regards your tender other half, you will always find a kind of opposition in me, that is, an opposition against you and a proposition for your wife.*

As always,

Your friend

⁂

Hetzendorf, 16 July 1823

My dear Ries,

How greatly pleased I was to receive your letter the day before yesterday. . . . By now the Variations probably have arrived. I could not write the dedication to your wife myself, since I do not know her name. Do it therefore yourself, on behalf of your and your wife's friend. Surprise your wife with it; the fair sex loves that. — Between you and me, the best thing possible is a combination of the surprising and the beautiful! . . . As far as the allegri di bravura *is concerned, I must have a look at yours. To be quite frank, I am no friend of that kind of thing since it unnaturally promotes mechanical playing. At least those I am familiar with do. I do not know yours yet, so I will enquire with . . ., with whom I would suggest you deal with caution. Could I not arrange various things for you here? These publishing presses, who are always trying to press you into service, pirate your works and you get nothing for it; it should be possible to devise some other arrangement. . . . I shall send you a few choruses; also, if necessary, I will compose a few new ones. This is what I really prefer. . . .*

Thank you for the payment for the Bagatelles[98]. *I am quite satisfied. — Do not give anything to the King of England. — Take whatever you can get for the Variations; I will be satisfied with anything. But I must stipulate that for the dedication to your wife no reward whatsoever will be accepted, other than a kiss, which I am to receive in London. You sometimes write about guineas and I receive only pounds sterling.*(1) *I hear, however, there is a difference. Do not be angry with a* pauvre musicien autrichien *about it. My situation really is still difficult. — I am also writing a new string quartet. Could one perhaps offer it to the musical or unmusical Jews in London? —* en vrai juif? —

Embracing you cordially,

your old friend

Beethoven

(1) For a 25 guinea fee Beethoven had been sent 26 pounds, 5 shillings. Accounts are transferred only in pounds.

***

5 September 1823

My dear, admirable Ries,

I still have no further news about the symphony. However, you can certainly expect . . . that it will soon be in London. Were I not so poor that I must live from my pen, I would not accept anything from the Philharmonic Society. As it is, I have to wait until the fee for the symphony has been transferred to me here. However, as a proof of my love and trust in the Society I have already sent off the new . . . overture[99] *to them. I leave it to the Society to decide what they will be able to arrange for the overture.*

My fine brother (Johann), who keeps a carriage, wanted to be pulled along by me as well and so offered this particular overture to a publisher — Boosey in London — without asking me. Say merely that, concerning the overture, my brother was mistaken. — He bought it from me in a profiteering spirit, I would say. O frater!

I have received nothing of your symphony dedicated to me. If I had not always regarded the dedication as a sort of challenge demanding an answer in kind, I would have dedicated a work to you long ago. But I have always felt that I had to see your work first. How glad I would be to demonstrate my gratitude to you in some way. I am, after all, deeply indebted to you for the loyalty and consideration you have so often shown me. If my upcoming treatment at the spa improves my health at all, I shall kiss your wife in London in 1824.

Ever yours,

Beethoven

Nikolaus Johann van Beethoven, Beethoven's youngest brother (1776-1848)

Vienna, 9 April 1825

My very dear Ries,

Quickly, just the most essential matters! In the score of the symphony I sent you (it was the Ninth, with chorus) there is, as far as I remember, in the first oboe, specifically bar 242

instead of

I have looked over all the instrumental parts (except the brass, which I have checked only here and there), and I believe they are more or less correct. I would gladly have sent you my own score(1)*, but I still have an academy concert ahead of me (and the manuscript is the only score I have). If only my health allows it, that is, because I must get out into the country soon: only in the country can I thrive at this time of year. — You will soon receive the* Opferlied[100]*, copied for the second time. Mark it immediately as having been corrected by me, so that it won't be used along with the one you have already. This will give you a sample of the miserable copyists I have had since Schlemmer's death. One can hardly rely on a single note. — Since you have received all the copied parts for the finale of the Symphony, I have sent you the vocal score as well. You can easily have them written into the score from the parts before the chorus enters, and where the singing begins it will be quite easy, if you are careful, to have the instrumental parts added above the vocal line in the score. It was not possible to have all this written out at the same time, and since it was done in a hurry, you would have been faced with nothing but errors from this copyist. I have sent you an Overture in C in 6/8 time,*[101] *which has not yet been published; the engraved parts you will receive by the next post. A Kyrie and a Gloria, two excellent pieces (from the* Messe solemnelle *in D major) and an Italian vocal duet are also on their way to you. You will also receive a grand march with chorus, well suited for a gala concert.*(2)) *A grand overture,*[102] *still unknown abroad, would also be available, but I think you will have enough with what I have sent. . . .*

I hope you are well, there in the Rhineland so dear to me.(3) *I wish you and your wife every happiness in life. To your father all my best wishes from your friend,*

Beethoven

(1) This passage concerns the intended performance of this

symphony — which Beethoven, however, did not send — at the music festival in Aachen. The local committee had also written to him directly, but had received only promises. At last I wrote and asked him, since I knew him and his scores so well, to send me the original score, and I would figure everything out. At the same time, knowing his constant need of money, I promised him a reward. They later handed me 40 Louis d'ors for him.

(2) Probably in the *Ruins of Athens*.

(3) When I left England, I moved to Godesberg, near Bonn, one of the loveliest regions on the Rhine. I had invited Beethoven to visit and urged him to live with me, there in his native country, for a while.

***

Epilogue

With this recollection of his pleasant stay in the beautiful town of Godesberg my late friend Ries finished his notes on Beethoven. His wish to welcome the Master there was not fulfilled. Beethoven died on 26 March 1827, in Vienna. The year previously Ries had moved from Godesberg and settled in Frankfurt am Main, which he did not leave again except for journeys to Italy, England, and France. Here he lived, tirelessly engaged in furthering his art, appreciated near and far, loved and honored by his friends. It is not without significance that memories of his great teacher were constantly at the center of everything he thought and did. Finally, having been asked so often, he decided to write them down. Why did the good humor in which they were started and for the most part completed have to give way so soon to illness and death for him, to melancholy grief for me!

Coblenz, May 1838

Wegeler

⁂

Ferdinand Ries

Musical score of Beethoven's "Die Klage" (see page 62)

SUPPLEMENT

Upon the Occasion of the Dedication of A Monument to Ludwig van Beethoven In Bonn, His Native Town

Foreword

Everything has its own time, during which it flourishes, then passes away; but whatever is noble, significant, and fertile in spirit endures beyond its time. It is now over seventy-four years since Beethoven was born in Bonn and over half a century since his mighty spirit began to spread its wings. Throughout the vicissitudes of his life, despite the disturbing effects of physical and mental distress, his artistic fame grew enormously. The world has now recognized the profundity of his spirit and bows before the power of his music. The statue, masterfully sculpted in bronze and placed in his beloved native city by artists and art lovers, will bear witness to this universal love and reverence for generations to come.

I am now the oldest living friend of the great Master, except for the venerable Great-grandfather Ries, who was born on 10 November 1755. I was in contact with Beethoven from his twelfth year until his death, and I feel unable to remain altogether silent on this happy occasion. It is now seven years since my friend Ferdinand Ries — who left this world all too soon — and I published, in Coblenz in 1838, a small collection of memories of Beethoven entitled *Biographical Notes on Ludwig van Beethoven*. I must say that my unforgettable friend Ries and I were mainly motivated by the idea of providing a respectful memorial to our departed friend. At the same time we wished to rectify errors and false ideas about the great man. We intended thereby to fulfill a duty of friendship to him.

This intention was fully appreciated. The little work was praised by many; it was also severely criticized; — much was learned from it; it also was translated into foreign languages, more or less completely and adequately. On reading these reviews, and also when further surveying our work and my collections, various remarks and additions came to mind. Perhaps they are not unworthy of seeing the light, like a bas relief on the memorial set up previously, as a supplement to the original.

Old age possesses its memories, youth its hopes.

On Beethoven's memorial, however, memory and hope should reach out and join hands.

Coblenz, August, 1845, at the close of his eightieth year.

Wegeler.

Supplement

Beethoven's name

The name is not the man, and yet it can become important for the man.

Ludwig van Beethoven was occasionally taken for a nobleman, because the Dutch *van* was equated with the German von. This happened for three years in Vienna. A lawsuit of Beethoven's was litigated for that long a period before the Landrecht court and was remanded to the city magistrate only after the error was discovered.[103]

(*Kölnische Zeitung*, 6 March 1844)

The house where Beethoven was born

Closer investigation, instigated by the teacher Dr. Hennes, into which house should be considered the birthplace of the great master, has shown at last that it is in fact, as I had said, the Graus house at Bonngasse 515, which now belongs to Dr. Schildt. An extensive discussion of this is to be found in the *Kölnische Zeitung*, in particular in the supplement to Issue no. 240 for 30 August 1838. The teacher Kneisel, who has a great reputation in Bonn, sets forth there clearly and convincingly the reasons for and against the idea that the Graus house is Beethoven's birthplace and proves the assumption correct. Subsequently Beethoven's parents lived in the house owned by a baker named Fischer at Rheingasse No. 934, which has often been erroneously taken for the house where he was born.

Beethoven's birthplace

The Fischer house

Beethoven's family

Beethoven's younger brother, Nicolaus Johanes, born in 1776, is still alive in Vienna, a rich man in comfortable circumstances. The foundations for this affluence had already been laid during Ludwig's lifetime. The son of his brother Carl (1774-1815) — Beethoven's nephew, ward, and subject of great concern — is said to be married and employed in Vienna at present.[104]

Beethoven's education and knowledge

Beethoven's father, who was so strict with his son, was rather too lenient with himself. In particular he was somewhat given to drink and was especially irascible in that condition. Young Ludwig did his exercises frequently in tears and was kept at them by the iron hand of his father. Apart from music he learned only reading, writing, arithmetic, and a little Latin at a public school. One admirer of his genius has turned him into a scholar who understood Latin, Italian, and French, as well as his native tongue. Beethoven was even alleged to have studied the philosophy of Kant.* The truth is that Beethoven never went to a gymnasium, understood only a few Latin idioms, and spoke French with difficulty. When private lectures on Kant were held in Vienna — arranged by Adam Schmidt, Wilhelm Schmidt, Hunczovsky, Göpfert, the Royal Physician, and several others — Beethoven did not want to attend even one of them,[105] not even when I tried to persuade him. He probably felt within himself a categorical imperative different from that of the great man from Königsberg. His knowledge was creation.

His deafness

All too early Beethoven's worst misfortune began, his deplorable hardness of hearing, which his beautiful letter to me on 29 June 1800 from Vienna bemoans so heartrendingly (p. 28). What Beethoven says there about his unhappy condition is further attested to in a letter on 13 October 1804 from our mutual friend Stephan von Breuning to me. To excuse his long silence Stephan von Breuning says: "The only friend here who goes back to my childhood is frequently and often the major reason that I am forced to neglect my absent

---

* Supplement to the *Kölner Zeitung* of 22 March 1835.

friends. You would not believe, dear Wegeler, what an indescribable and, I should say, truly dreadful impact the loss of his hearing has had on him. Imagine the feeling of being unhappy — and with such a vehement nature as his. Add to this his shyness, distrust (often of his best friends) and general indecisiveness! For the most part, except for the occasional moments when his original affection expresses itself freely, association with him is a real strain, and one can never be quite off one's guard. From May until the beginning of this month we lived in the same house, and early on I invited him to stay in my flat. He had just barely moved in when he became violently ill. The illness threatened to become really dangerous but finally passed into a lingering, intermittent fever. The worry and the nursing were a considerable strain on me. Now he is quite well again. He lives on the ramparts, and I live in a house newly built by Prince Esterhazy in front of the Alster Barracks.* Since January I have kept my own household, including a sixty-six year old cook, so he eats lunch with me daily. "

His financial affairs

Only in his last years did Beethoven appear to have been living in reduced circumstances, even though he complained of this much earlier. That this was not always the case is

* The street built within the last few years and bearing Beethoven's name runs straight behind this house, and the one known as the Schwarz-Spanier, where Beethoven died.

proved by the following lines, which he enclosed with a letter to me from Lenz von Breuning in May, 1797:

"God bless you, my dear friend! I owe you a letter, which you shall have very soon, as well as my latest compositions. I am well and, I might say, always improving. If you think anyone would be pleased, give them my regards. Farewell, and do not forget your L. v. Beethoven."

His comfortable financial circumstances lasted until 1800, as he told me himself happily in great detail (p. 28).

Unfortunately this had already changed for the worse by 1806. Stephan v. Breuning wrote to me in October that year: "Beethoven is at present with Prince Lichnowsky in Silesia and will not come back before the end of this month. His circumstances now are not the best, as his opera* has been only rarely performed, through the intrigues of his enemies, and has therefore not brought him anything. He is in a very melancholy mood for the most part, and to judge from his letters the stay in the country has not cheered him up."

His illnesses

Illness Beethoven unfortunately knew all too well, as is clearly demonstrated above (p. 39), contrary to Ignatz von Seyfried's contention. The seeds of his disorders, his hearing problems, and the dropsy which finally killed him, already lay within my friend's ailing body in 1796 (p. 28). The frequent interruptions of any regular regime were bound to aggravate this basic infirmity.

---

* *Fidelio*

However, Beethoven was also susceptible to other illnesses which could not be ascribed to the same source. Stephan von Breuning wrote to me in March, 1808: "Beethoven almost lost a finger because of a parasitic infection. However, he is reasonably well again. He was thus spared a great misfortune which, on top of his hardness of hearing, would have put an end to any good spirits completely, which are rare enough as it is."[106]

He himself complains (p. 136): "Now, I am not well from the many grievances I have suffered, and even my eyes are sore."[107]

And of course Breuning's letter quoted earlier speaks of the severe illness which had overcome Beethoven in von Breuning's flat.

By and large Beethoven lived very moderately, and as far as I know, not one of his friends and acquaintances ever saw him intoxicated. Dr. Waurauch's[108] statement that Dr. Malfatti had prescribed iced punch for him when he suffered from dropsy because as an old friend he knew Beethoven's strong taste for alcoholic beverages, is therefore completely unfounded. (*Frankfurter Conversationsblatt* No. 192, 1842.) Causes for dropsy were unfortunately abundant. — The accusation — which Livius had long ago leveled against musicians in Rome, when he called them *vini avidum ferme genus*,* and with which I frequently teased my friend — should be treated with considerable reservation.

* Livius, *Historiarum* lib. IX. Cap. 30

His marriage intentions

It does indeed seem that at one time in his life Beethoven entertained the thought of marriage, having often been involved in love affairs, as these *Notes* point out (p. 105).[109] Several readers have noticed, as I had, the urgency with which Beethoven in his letter on 10 May 1810 asked me to obtain his baptismal certificate. He insisted on underwriting all my expenses, even the travel costs from Coblenz to Bonn, and gave detailed instructions on what to look out for to be certain the certificate I obtained was the correct one (p. 45).[110]

I found the solution to the puzzle in a letter from my brother-in-law, Stephan von Breuning, written to me three months later. He says: "Beethoven tells me at least once every week that he wants to write to you. However, I believe his marriage plans have fallen through, and therefore he no longer feels such an urge to thank you for obtaining his baptismal certificate."

Thus Beethoven had still not given up the thought of marriage in his thirty-ninth year.

A printer's error in the *Notes*

"Graf von Marienstadt" (p.55)[111] should read: "Graf von Marienrode". Therefore, the famous author of the classic work on economics (1830, 2 vols.), Karl August Freiherr von Malchus, who died at the age of seventy on 24 October 1830, was also one of Beethoven's closer acquaintances.

Beethoven's opinion of Mozart certainly reflects on both of them. Ries asserts that of all composers Beethoven thought most highly of Mozart and Handel, "and then Seb. Bach. If I found him with music in his hand or if anything lay open on his desk, it was sure to be a composition by one of these heroes" (p. 73).[112] Now L. Rellstab (*Weltgegenden*, vol. 3) tells us that during a visit where opera libretti for Beethoven were discussed, Beethoven made the following statement: "I am not too particular about the genre if the material attracts me. But I must be able to approach it with love and tenderness. I could not compose operas like *Don Giovanni* and *Figaro*. I have an aversion to that."[113] Rellstab recognized this, certainly with justice, as a confession of the great Master about the basic difference between himself and Mozart. Beethoven prefers the transcendental; Mozart is greatest when he reaches into the full, sensuous, natural life, penetrating right to the follies and passions of the human heart.

This much can be accepted. However, what should one say to a statement by the Marquise of Abrantes? First she raises Beethoven above Raphael and Michaelangelo, Dante, and Shakespeare. Then she continues (*Memoires*, p. 29):[114]

> Beethoven did not love Mozart. I cannot forgive him for that. It is a fault! That is, for me, something which reveals a lack of taste. — His reason for condemning *Don Giovanni* is sheer buffoonery. He claimed that Mozart should not have prostituted his talent (that's his word) on such a scandalous subject.

So then, the serious Beethoven, the greatest admirer of

Mozart, stooped to "buffoonery", indeed to "buffoonery" at his idol's expense? — He spoke of prostitution, our noble, highly proper master? — Are the requirements of propriety set higher in France or in Germany? — Who does in fact reveal a "lack of taste" — Beethoven or Madame Abrantes?

Concern for his pupil Ries

Ries recounts an incident (p. 84)[115] which demonstrates Beethoven's rash manner and inflexible behavior even toward friends when he thought them guilty of something. In this case Ries lost the most promising prospect of a position in Cassel which Beethoven himself had refused.

But, to Beethoven's credit it must be said that both he and his friend Breuning went to much trouble at that time to improve Ries's situation. "However, it is most difficult," as Breuning wrote to me, "to comply with both the father's wishes (Ries's father) and our own, and to combine our concern for the son's livelihood with the possibility of advancing him in his art. Beethoven is also now often distracted by his present situation, which obliges him to frequent the circles of the great families. — From my own experience I might add Vienna is no longer the place it was. The war has had an immense influence; the great families are curtailing their expenses in those things where they formerly were wont to be generous. And, of course, this is where one first gets a start, etc." Thus it was very probably more a question of the times than of a lack of zeal on Beethoven's part if his excellent pupil (p. 101)[116] did not readily attain the independence he desired.

His travels

"Beethoven hardly traveled at all," according to Ries (p. 96).[117] In our times, when the ease of travel and consequently also the desire for it grows every year, this would be somewhat incomprehensible. But even artists traveled much less thirty, forty years ago than they do nowadays. However, even Beethoven's life was not entirely devoid of travel. In January, 1796, the two elder brothers von Breuning, Christoph and Stephan, met him at Nuremberg on the way back to Vienna. Where he had been is not stated. Possibly Berlin.* Since none of the three had identity cards for Vienna, they were detained in Linz. I intervened for them in Vienna, and they were soon allowed to continue their travels. Later Beethoven also considered a journey to Italy. The war may have prevented it. Who knows what glorious and fruitful, even life-long, impression the lovely South might have left on the artist's soul? After all, his favorite models, Handel and Mozart, had also, to their renown, traveled in Italy at an early age. It was certainly unfortunate that Beethoven did not carry out this plan. Later on, of course, his miserable deafness prevented him more and more from moving beyond his usual circle. The fact, however, that travel did have a beneficial effect on him is clear from passages in Stephan von Breuning's letters to his mother, which I shall quote here:

"From Nuremberg Beethoven traveled always in our

---

* Cf. p. 96[118], where it indicates that he had been visiting King Friedrich Wilhelm II.

company. Naturally, three natives of Bonn together aroused the attention of the police, who were sure they had discovered something. I do not think that one could find a less dangerous man than Beethoven. " (Letter from Stephan von Breuning to his mother, January, 1796.) Beethoven also never came into contact with the police, even though he is supposed to have drawn the attention of those authorities to himself with sharp criticism of administrative regulations and with his democratic ideas. (Cf. the story of the *Sinfonia eroica*, which first bore the title *Bonaparte*; p. 68.)[119]

The same Stephan von Breuning wrote his brother and myself on 23 November 1796 from Mergentheim: "I do not know whether Lenz (the youngest of the brothers von Breuning) has written anything about Beethoven; if he has not, here is the news. I saw him while still in Vienna, and in my opinion, which Lenz also confirms, the journey (or perhaps the outpouring of friendship upon his return!) has made him more stable, or actually a better judge of men, and has convinced him of the rarity and value of good friends. A hundred times, my dear Wegeler, he has wished you were back with us, and he regrets nothing more than that he did not follow many of your suggestions."

Stephan von Breuning also wrote his mother: "I have written Wegeler that since the beginning of this year (1811), I have been keeping my own household with a sixty-six year old cook. Beethoven now eats with me. When he is not here, as was the case during the summer and will probably be again soon since he is supposed to travel to Italy, I eat alone."

This journey was not undertaken.

Immediately after the mutual journey mentioned above, the youngest of the Breunings wrote to me in January, 1796: "Beethoven is back again. He played in Romberg's Academy concert. He is still the old Beethoven, and I am glad that he and the Rombergs still get on so well. Once he almost had a falling out with them; I played the mediator, more or less successfully. In general he now sets great store by me."

General Remarks

Here follows an amusing letter from Beethoven to Stephan von Breuning, which may also serve to throw proper light on the relationship between the two:

(Probably 1820)

You, my esteemed friend, are overburdened, and so am I. And I am still not quite well. — I would have invited you to a meal before now. However, I am going around with a number of people whose most inspiring muse is the cook, and since inspired works are not to be found in their own spirit cellars, they seek them out in other kitchens and other cellars.[120] *— You would not be particularly well served by their company. However, this will soon change. Do not practice Czerny's studies for the pianoforte for the time being; I shall get detailed information about other exercises within the next few days.*

Here is the fashion journal I promised your wife, and something for your children. I can always pass on copies of this journal to you. And if there is anything else you could possibly wish from me, you have only to let me know.

In love and respect,

Your friend

Beethoven

*I hope we will be seeing each other soon.**

⁂

Gerhard von Breuning, Stephan von Breuning's only son, wrote to me just this year:

One of Beethoven's most cherished wishes was to possess Handel's complete works. When these arrived during his last illness as a present from England, I had to stack them all up on his bed against the wall — I think about fifty volumes — where he kept them almost all day long, always leafing through them, beside himself with joy, and endlessly praising that great master.[121]

*I was using Pleyel's pianoforte studies; but with this, as with all the others, he was not satisfied.*** *He said to me once when I was sitting at his bedside: "I felt like writing a set of pianoforte exercises myself once, but never found the time for it; I would have written something quite unconventional though." He then promised my father that he would provide a manual of exercises for me. Some time later he sent me Clementi's, which was not available at the time, with the following note:*

"Dear Werther,

At long last I can carry out what I carried on about. Here are

---

* The original of this letter is in the possession of von Breuning's widow in Vienna.

** See the letter cited above on p. 157.

the Clementi exercises promised for Gerhard. If he practices them according to my instruction, they certainly will produce good results.

I do hope to see you very soon and embrace you fondly.

Yours,

Beethoven "

These are but bits and pieces, remembered from a friendship in years gone by and solemnly offered here at the foot of this memorial, which is intended to proclaim Beethoven's artistic fame to the world. And yet, small as they are, these postscripts to what has been related do not seem insignificant to me, because everything is valuable to me that summons up before my inner self the presence of my friend and his noble qualities.

The sculptor has represented for us in bronze the glorious form of the master of sound, towering above a base of the most solid granite. I have dwelt more on the man, the friend. His works are admired by the world, and in their radiant character we can glimpse the soul from which they emerged.

Well, nothing can or need be added to the works, which will perpetuate Beethoven's fame forever. But I can still limn a few more features on the portrait of the man, the loyal friend.

Here, then, are a letter from Stephan von Breuning and a page from an autograph album.

Of course, these are only isolated outpourings of a great soul. But who can remain unmoved when Beethoven as a twenty-six year old young man confesses to his friend Lenz von Breuning that the union of truth and beauty is the highest ideal for a wise and sensitive man![122] — And he remained true to this belief throughout his life, through happiness and misfortune. His works openly proclaim to the world what he confided to his intimate friend. His own words could serve as inscription on the spiritual memorial a friend's hand has endeavored to erect here:

Truth and Beauty Joined

⁂

A letter from Beethoven to St. v. Breuning sent with his portrait:

Miniature portrait of Beethoven on ivory by Christian Hornemann, 1803

(Undated)*

Behind this painting, my dear, good Stephan, may all that has happened between us for some time be hidden forever. — I know I have torn open your heart. My own emotion, which surely you must have noticed, has

---

* The original of this letter is in the possession of von Breuning's widow in Vienna.

punished me severely enough. It was not malice that motivated me against you; no, or I would no longer be worthy of your friendship. Passion worked on both our sides —yet, distrust of you erupted within me. Men came between us who will never be worthy of you or me. —My portrait has long been intended for you; you know that I had always intended it for someone. To whom could I give it with such a warm heart as to you, faithful, good, noble Steffen! — Forgive me if I have hurt you; I myself have suffered just as much. When I did not see you around me for such a long time, I realized all the more sharply how dear you are to my heart and ever will be. — Surely you will rush into my arms again with the same trust as before!

⁂

With this letter all the quarrels, which, as Beethoven's letters to Ries clearly demonstrate, were frequent between the friends, seem to have come to an end. "Steffen," wrote Beethoven, "has really become a good, wonderful boy, who knows a few things and has his heart in the right place" (p. 30).

And yet the two were separated so often! Steffen writes on 10 January 1809: "I have not seen Beethoven for over three months. He has during this time written me in a rather friendly way but has not visited me again; I do not know the reason why."

⁂

Beethoven wrote into the autograph album belonging to Lenz von Breuning:

Truth exists for the wise;
Beauty for a feeling heart.
Both are meant for each other.[123]

Dear, worthy Breuning,

Never will I forget the time which I have spent with you, both in Bonn and here. Preserve your friendship for me, in return you will always find me the same.*

Vienna, 1797
on the 1st of October

Your true friend,
L. v. Beethoven. "

(The album is in my possession.)

***

From these outpourings we can see that Beethoven was always in the most intimate relationship with the von Breuning family. Stephan von Breuning indeed especially deserved this friendship. He had a most noble nature, which can be seen very clearly in his behavior toward his dearly beloved mother,** his sister, brothers, and other relatives. These qualities have been handed on to his children. Stephan's son, Dr. Gerhard von Breuning, is well known in Vienna and beyond as a doctor and surgeon. Since a talent for music runs in the family, one of the daughters has tried her hand at

---

* Lenz von Breuning, as the youngest of the three brothers, was closest to Beethoven in age.

** Frau von Breuning (born 1750, died at Coblenz in 1838), to whom Beethoven also owed a great deal in his youth. (p. 15).[124]

composition as an amateur, not without success. In this family, then, Beethoven's memory lives on.

⁂

Finally, here is also a little offering for the artist, a romance composed by Beethoven and hitherto unpublished. It was found in Stephan von Breuning's family papers and sent to me with the following title to use as I thought fit:

Upon Learning of Lydia's Infidelity

A Song

set to music

by

Ludwig van Beethoven

(The poem is taken from the French)

The original text, as far as I know, is taken from the opera *Le Secret* by Solie.[125] Beethoven, however, set the melody to a German text, finishing it in May of 1806, according to the handwriting and to changes in Stephan von Breuning's manuscript.* The composition of the ballad, then, falls still within our Master's earlier period, although several knowledgeable judges of Beethoven's work place it on the same level as the best of his work in this style at a later period.

This is the poem:

---

* At the same time I happened to translate this same ballad along with several other songs from the same opera for Simrock, my fondly remembered friend, who then published them.

Ballad

Feelings Upon Lydia's Infidelity

So the last gleam of hope has now declined.
She broke her vows; fickle is her mind.
And now I lose, to infinite unrest,
All consciousness that I was once so blessed.

What did I say! Still her charms enslave me.
No power can turn, no resolution save me
Yet when I reach the brink of wild despair
Sweet memories stay with me there.

Ah, gentle hope to me once more returning
Do thou revive the flame within me burning
Though love's sufferings indeed are great
Still he who loves would never change his fate.

And thou who does my love so true disdain
Thy image will within my heart remain.
I could not hate thee, no but love thee more.
Forget thee? Not till this life of woe be o'er.

⁂

The small worth of these additional remarks I would not deny, but the thought that everything here is an offering to Beethoven's admirers led me on. Thus came into being this little portion of some future biography, which only a true musician will be able to write. Beethoven's entire soul lives on in his works; all his joys and sorrows have been consigned to his art. His music is his real biography, the true and imperishable story of what he strove for and what he accomplished, written for all people and all times.

Finally, I feel justified in claiming also for these additional remarks the same credibility, other sources to the contrary, which was generally accorded the *Notes* themselves when they first appeared.

And now may these modest words of fond remembrance mingle with the noise of ceremonial rejoicing, which is not only to be indulged but also to be cheerfully taken up.

⁂

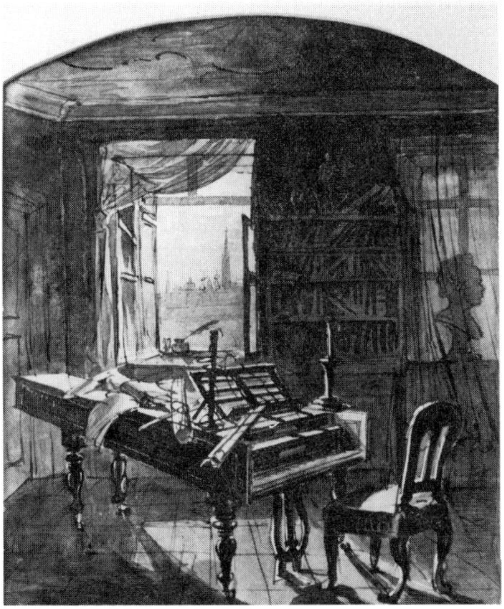

Beethoven's study in the Schwarzspanierhaus, 1827

Empfindungen bei Lydien's Untreue

von

BONN bei N. SIMROCK.
Eigenthum des Verlegers.

L. van BEETHOVEN.

Das Gedicht ist nach dem Französischen.

Ha! holde Hoffnung kehr' zu mir zu - rü - cke, reg' all mein Feu - er auf mit einem
Bli - cke. der Liebe Lei - den seien noch so gross, wer liebt, wer liebt, — fühlt ganz un -
glücklich nie sein Loos! Und du, die treu - er Lieb' mit Kränkung
loh - net, Fürcht' nicht die Brust, in der dein Bild noch wohnet, Dich hassen könn - te nie dies fühlend
Herz, vergessen, vergessen? eh' er - liegt es seinem Schmerz.
p
cres
sf
f
tr
4424

Notes

The following notes are a complete translation of the annotations by Dr. Alfred C. Kalischer to his edition of the ***Biographische Notizen über Ludwig van Beethoven*** by Wegeler and Ries, second edition, published 1906 in Berlin. The numbers, which appear in the text as boldface superscripts, are in the sequence and location given by Kalischer in his edition. The very few notes which are not translated refer either to minor variants in the German text or to page numbers in Kalischer's editions. Otherwise the translation is true to the meticulous accuracy and idiosyncracies of the original.

1. Despite this quite unequivocal, incontestable claim of Franz Wegeler, the creditable Beethoven biographer A.W. Thayer has attempted to prove that Beethoven's relationship with Wegeler and the whole von Breuning circle did not begin until after the pilgrimage to Mozart, this is, after July 1787 — an effort which of course was bound to fail. Already in 1890 Wegeler's grandson, the independently wealthy Koblenzer Carl Wegeler, successfully rebuffed Thayer's puzzling assertion in the *Kölnische Zeitung* (no. 143, May 24, 1890). Printing the complete version of a letter presented only in fragmentary form in this Beethoven book, he rests his case with complete justification on the following sentence of this letter of Beethoven to Wegeler: "Oh, Wegeler, my only consolation is that you have known me since my childhood." This letter will be printed in its complete form in the appropriate place (note 20, below). Even Dr. H. Deiters, the knowledgeable and perceptive editor of Thayer's Beethoven biography, finds himself forced to concede in the 2nd edition of 1901 (I, 206): "Also all the additional reports gain meaning and fall into place only if one assumes that Beethoven had found acceptance in the von Breuning household as early as his boyhood days. The editor [Dr. Deiters] thus believes that in this matter he must differ from Thayer's opinion."

I myself can and must at this point introduce in favor of F. Wegeler's incontestable assertion yet a few additional pieces of evidence which I found in a little-known publication. In the year 1839 F.G. Wegeler celebrated the fiftieth anniversary of his doctorate. For this celebration a *festschrift* was compiled which consisted of a sizeable number of contributions in both poetry and prose, and which was printed in its entirety. There is a biographical sketch, "Franz Gerhard Wegeler," probably written by his son, Dr. Julius Wegeler. Here one finds (page 8):

> At this point one must also remember the noteworthy relationship in which Wegeler had stood since 1782 to his great countryman, the composer Ludwig van Beethoven. This relationship had been formed between the two youths in Bonn and then cemented through common experience, sufferings, and joys in their mutual development as well as through their association with the von Breuning family, with whom they were intimately connected. Up until September 1787, when Wegeler went to Vienna, this association continued uninterrupted and then was resumed with equal warmth after his return to Bonn in 1789 and up to the time of Beethoven's departure for Vienna at the end of 1791. In Vienna the friends came together again with undiminished feelings and a day rarely went by on which they did not see one another.

The fact that Wegeler had been friends with Beethoven since boyhood days is powerfully celebrated in this *Wegleriana* in the fifth and sixth strophes of a festive poem in classical form:

> Him today I joyfully greet
> With the powerful greeting of the ancients,
> Greet him with splendid Hellenic rhythms,
> Bring him homage with the echoing sounds
> Of the festival ode.
>
> Proudly must the chorus sing
> Of the understanding friend of art
> Who once listened to Beethoven's lofty muse,
> Almost while still in the cradle,
> And early prophesied the future splendor.

It should be mentioned that Wegeler, born on August 22, 1765, was more than five years older than Beethoven.

2. Here Wegeler writes that the day of baptism is "usually the actual day of birth or certainly the day after." This is an unhappy error. If this were true all those who assume that December 17 is the composer's birthday, as Wegeler himself later does, would be correct. This Rhenish custom is in fact a curious matter, as I have already demonstrated (compare the editor's article "When Was Beethoven Born?" in the Sunday Supplement to the *Vossische Zeitung* of January 11, 1891). On inquiring into this Bonn custom I have heard the most varied contradictions. From a Catholic friend born in Aachen, a portrait painter by trade, I learned that in accordance with Catholic custom in all the districts and regions known to him, the newborn child is usually baptized at the latest on the third day after its birth. That arises from the Catholic belief that the child, if it were to die unbaptized, would not be able to partake of heaven. My informant knows no example from his area of the baptism of a newborn child on the first day.

3. Dr. Deiters, the editor of A.W. Thayer's biography of Beethoven, points out in the 2nd edition (1901, p. 107) that Wegeler's presentation of the facts is not precise. The maiden name of the mother — Johann van Beethoven's wife — which Wegeler states as Westorffs, is not given in the *Ehrenbreitstein Parish Book* of December 1746; Westorf is the name of the godmother. Dr. Deiters cites the entry in the Parish Book as follows: "19 nata et 20ma renata (= baptized) est Maria Magdalena Keverichs, D^{ni} Henrici Keverich coqui primarii Em^{smi} et Mariae Catharinae cjugum Legitima filia, eam de sacro fonte Levantibus D^{na} Maria Magdalena Westorfs de Confluentia [Coblenz], et D^{no} Mauritio Wisdorff [sic] itidem de Confluentia."

According to this it is not true that the day of the baptism coincides with the day of birth.

4. As Dr. Deiters has established, this should read: "Henrici Keferich et annae clarae [not Mariae] Westorffs filiam legitimam." "If the Bonn Parish Book calls her a born Westorffs, then it seems that at the issuance of the daughter's baptismal certificate for the purpose of her wedding in Bonn, the same erroneous reading of the

birth certificate prevailed as in the communication of the information to Wegeler." Cf.note 3.

5. To be precise this should read "baptized" on April 2, 1769.

6. This is not clear. Even in the Thayer-Deiters version — "the wife of the locksmith Jean Courtin" — the matter does not become clear.

7. It is incomprehensible that Wegeler can here so positively assert that Ludwig van Beethoven was born on December 17, since the document that follows merely says "baptizatus est Ludovicus": Ludwig was baptized. I have already advanced the argument above that it cannot be claimed with plausibility that Catholic children in the Rhineland were baptized one day after birth. Up to three days may elapse after the birth. The peremptory passage in the *Conversation Books* (no. 63, leaf 6b) of December 1823 remains all the more in force. There Beethoven's nephew writes: "Today is December 15 and that is when you were born, so far as I could see; however, I could not vouch for whether it might be the 15th or the 17th, since one cannot rely on the baptismal certificate, and anyway I only read about this once, in *Janus*, when I was still at your place. I already thought about it yesterday and at some length, but the unpleasantness that occurred yesterday made it inopportune to mention it." If one compares this with the fact that even Dr. Hennes in his article "Beethoven's Birthplace" (printed in Thayer-Deiters' first and second editions) states: "Beethoven was born in Bonn in the year 1770, in the middle of December, probably on December 15," where two days before the baptism are assumed, one can thus assert in bringing this discussion to a close: the 15th of December is far more probable as Beethoven's birthday than the 16th or even the 17th of December.

8. [Missing in Kalischer's edition of 1906.]

9. General material and historical information on the legendary descent of Beethoven from King Frederick William II of Prussia has been published in my article "Beethoven in Berlin" in the November 1886 issue of the journal *Nord und Süd* (Breslau). Although the Englishman who would have Beethoven be a natural son of Frederick the Great has well earned Wegeler's ridicule because of

his ignorance of chronology, he however deserves some credit for being the first and only one to name Frederick II as Beethoven's natural father. For only very recently did I find in Beethoven's *Conversation Books* a noteworthy confirmation of the fact that in the composer's most intimate circle the belief was cherished that he was a natural son of Frederick the Great. In a *Conversation Book* from 1820 (no. 22) in just the place in which Karl Bernhard sings Napoleon's praises to Beethoven, this author and editor writes, among other things (leaf 39a):

> Napoleon was a man of arts and sciences.
> In the Encyclopedia [Conversations-Lexicon] it says that you are a natural son of the great Frederick.

And immediately thereafter Hofrat Peters writes:

> H. v. Janitschek is of the opinion that you love Frederick the Great so much because he is supposed to be your father.
> Such errors must however be corrected. You don't need to borrow anything from Frederick.
> (Bernhard 39b). Someone should put an article in the *Allgemeine Zeitung*.

10. The operetta *L'Amore Artigiano* , with music by Florian Leopold Gassmann († 1774 in Vienna) was performed in Bonn in the arrangement by C.G. Neefe.

11. Tobias Friedr. Pfeiffer was certainly succeeded by the court organist Egidius von der Eeden as the young Beethoven's teacher for piano and organ.

12. What is here said about Chr. Gottlob Neefe, however, is not to the point. Beethoven, as he himself acknowledged, owed much to this extraordinary teacher, particularly in composition instruction. Also, it is sufficiently well known how clearly Neefe recognized Beethoven's genius in *statu nascenti.*

12a. Wegeler here cites the first edition of von Seyfried's book. In the second edition, January 1853, edited by H.H. Pierson (Mannsfeld), these words are followed by: "and conferred on him the status of court organist, along with several years leave and free passage to Vienna" (Appendix, p. 4).

13. The friendship and respect which Beethoven felt for the

Rombergs in general and for the cellist Bernhard Romberg in particular, even when he was already at the zenith of his fame as a composer, becomes clear from Beethoven's first and only letter to Romberg, which the editor published several years ago. See *New Beethoven Letters,* Berlin 1902, page 58f. Bernhard Romberg died long after Beethoven, in Hamburg in 1841. Pleyel, also mentioned here, is Haydn's pupil Ignaz Pleyel († 1831). The time of the anecdote is the year 1791. Cf. A.W. Thayer's *Beethoven* I, 242; 2nd ed., revised by H. Deiter, Berlin 1901.

14. This cantata has in the meantime appeared in print. It is the Funeral Cantata on the Death of Emperor Joseph II, which had its first performance in Vienna in November 1884. Ed. Hanslick first brought the discovery of the cantata to the attention of the music world. This cantata, as well as the other, written on the occasion of the accession of Leopold II to the imperial throne, has been printed in the supplementary volume to the large edition of Beethoven's works by Breitkopf and Härtel.

15. A piano arrangement by Dulcken of the music to a Ritterballet was published in 1872 by Rieter Biedermann in Leipzig. The music appeared in its original form in the Breitkopf & Härtel *Complete Works* in series 25, no. 286.

16. These are, of course, by no means all the compositions dating from the period of Beethoven's life in Bonn. Many others can be added to these, most of which have by now been printed. In this connection one should study the noteworthy chapter in Thayer's *Beethoven*, "What Did Beethoven Compose in Bonn?" (I, 231-241) and especially the creditable enlargement of this chapter by H. Deiters (2nd ed., pp. 272-313).

16a. The words are from Horace's *Satires* (Liber I, Sat. IX, verse 20). In complete form:

> Demitto auriculas, ut iniquae mentis asellus,
> Cum gravius dorso subiit onus.

17. This can only be understood, however, regarding Beethoven's letters to Wegeler and Ries; other letters from the master had already found their way to public attention. One has only to be reminded of Beethoven's interesting letter to Abbé Stadler on Mozart, which the first small Beethoven biography by Schlosser

(1828) presents in facsimile. One thinks further of the not insignificant number of Beethoven's letters to the music dealer Hofmeister & Kühnel in Leipzig (later C.F. Peters), which were published in 1837 — that is, before the appearance of the *Biographical Notes* — in the *Neue Zeitschrift für Musik* under the editorship of R. Schumann.

18. This extremely important letter belongs to the following year (1801), however, as Thayer has already convincingly demonstrated (*Beethovens Leben* II, 156). — Thus I wrote in the first edition of this annotated reprint. After renewed examination, however, I have arrived at a new opinion. In this matter I now stand with Wegeler, Nohl and Schindler, all of whom place this letter in the year 1800. Compare the notes to this letter (no. 36) in [Kalischer's] *Beethoven's Complete Letters*, I, 51.

19. That the artists performing in the string quartet at Prince Carl Lichnowsky's are listed differently by different Beethoven biographers is connected with the circumstance that these quartet performances later alternated with those at Count (later Prince) A. Razumovsky's so that the artists from the Lichnowsky Quartet became confused with those from the Razumovsky Quartet. The confusion was not lessened by the fact that some of these artists also participated in the house orchestra of Prince von Lobkowitz. Schindler names the members of the Lichnowsky Quartet, mentioned here by Wegeler, as J. Schuppanzigh, the violist Franz Weiss, and the two cellists Anton Krafft and his son Nicholas Krafft (I, 35), whereas A.W. Thayer names Louis Sina as the second violin (I, 275). — The cellist Linke, whom Wegeler problematically introduces, does not in any case belong here. As members of the Razumovsky "Model Quartet" Schindler lists (I, 38): Schuppanzigh first violin, Sina second violin, Weiss viola, and Linke cello. — Despite this peremptory presentation Thayer's own more recent investigations yielded a different result. The name of Sina, the man who was later so zealously active in the introduction of Beethoven's music in Paris (Sina, † 1857 at Boulogne sur mer) is completely absent in Thayer. He explains that in addition to Count Razumovsky, who usually played the second violin himself, Maysede probably stepped in from time to time (III, 48). Anyway, this holds good *non liquet*. In any case, we have here solid testimony that the later Schuppanzigh

String Quartet consisted of the other artists of the Razumovsky Quartet, with the exception of Sina. The part of the second violin was not infrequently played by Beethoven's youthful friend Karl Holz. Before the premier of the first of the late quartets (E-flat, Op. 127), Beethoven directed the following order to the performers:

> *My dear friends, each person is herewith given his own part and is bound by oath, that is to say he pledges on his honor, to perform at his best, to distinguish himself, and to strive for mutual excellence. This paper is to be signed by each one of you who is to take part in this endeavor.*
>
> *Beethoven*
>
> *Schuppanzigh, m.p.*
> *Weiss, m.p.*
> *Linke, m.p.*
> *The accursed cello of the great master.*
> *Holz, m.p.*
> *Last, however, only in signing.*

(Cf. Schindler II, 113). Karl Holz later also played the first violin in August 1825 in the A Minor Quartet .

20. This letter has attained a larger significance in Beethoven's biography because a passage is found there that offers unmistakeable evidence for the fact that Beethoven's friendship with Wegeler reaches back long, long before 1787, so that Thayer's assertion that Beethoven did not become acquainted with Wegeler and the whole von Breuning circle until after his trip to Vienna, is also deeply shaken by this letter. Wegeler's grandson, Herr Karl Wegeler, with the help of this letter (which he published in the *Coblenzer Zeitung* of May 20, 1890) victoriously fought his case against Thayer (compare the article in the *Kölnische Zeitung*, no. 143, second morning edition of May 24, 1890). This very important letter runs as follows:

My dearest, my best friend! What a detestable picture have you shown me of myself! Oh, I realize I do not deserve your friendship, you are so noble, so thoughtful, and this is the first time that I may not stand near you, I have fallen far beneath you. Oh, for weeks I have caused distress to my best and noblest friend. You think that I have lost some of my goodness of heart. But thank Heaven! — it was no intentional, premeditated evil on my part which caused me to behave so. It was my unforgiveable levity which did not permit me to see the matter in its true light. O how ashamed I am both on your behalf and on mine! I almost no longer trust myself to plead with you again for your friendship. Oh, Wegeler, my only consolation is that you have known me almost since my childhood! And nevertheless — oh, let me say it myself — I was really always good and made the effort to be upright and honorable in my dealings. How else could you have loved me? Can I then in so short a time have changed so terribly and so to my disadvantage? Impossible! Can my feelings for the great and the good suddenly have been extinguished? No, Wegeler, dearest and best friend. But venture once more to throw yourself completely into the arms of your B. Build upon the good qualities which you otherwise have found in him. I promise you that the pure temple of holy friendship you will thereupon erect will endure firmly, eternally. No mischance, no storm will be able to shake its foundation — firm — eternal — our friendship — forgiveness — forgetfulness — revival of our dying, sinking friendship. Oh, Wegeler, do not turn away this hand of reconciliation, put yours into mine. Oh, God — but nothing more. I myself am coming to you and will throw myself into your arms and will plead for the lost friend and you will return to me, your penitent one who loves you and will never forget you.

Beethoven.

I have just now received your letter because I have just now returned home.

Even Dr. H. Deiters has been convinced by Karl Wegeler's arguments: He declares, among other things, in the second edition of Thayer's *Beethoven* (I, 206) in the notes: "The editor thus believes that in this matter he must differ from Thayer's opinion."

21. For example, with Hofrat Peters, with the lawyer Dr. Joh. Bapt. Bach, with Zmeskal von Domanovecz, among others.

22. This is Kaspar Karl von Beethoven, the father of Beethoven's famous nephew, also named Karl.

23. However, in the second edition of this book by von Seyfried, *Ludwig van Beethoven Studies* (1853), it is stated (Appendix, p. 26): "Beethoven knew neither stinginess (!) nor extravagance."

24. That was on the occasion of Beethoven's first public appearance as a pianist and composer, in March 1795. The Piano Concerto in C Major, which he then performed in the Burg Theater, did not appear in print until 1801 as Opus 15. A. Schindler is mistaken in his observation that this concerto, dedicated to the Princess von

Odescalchi, had its first performance in the Kärnthner-thor Theater in the Spring of 1801. This place in Wegeler's notes supports the chronology given in Nottebohm and Thayer.

25. The world famous Dr. Peter Frank was born on March 14, 1745 in Rothalben in the Palatinate and died in Vienna on April 24, 1821. In 1795 he came to Vienna, the second time in 1808. He was the founder of the field of public health.

26. Seyfried, however, contradicts himself. For prior to this pronouncement, he has it quite otherwise (appendix, page 9): "Gradually other bodily ills also arose, forcing the once thoroughly healthy, robust man to seek medical assistance."

27. Correctly, Baron Joh. Bapt. — von Pasqualati (= Pasquillati, Pascolati), in whose house on the Mölker-Bastei Beethoven lodged so frequently, that it gave rise to the Baron's characteristic remark: "The rooms are not to be rented; Beethoven will come back."

28. To this famous physician, Prof. Dr. J.A. Schmidt, Beethoven in 1802 gratefully dedicated the great Septet (Op. 20), which he himself had arranged as a trio for piano, clarinet (violin), and cello. He attended the composer during his grave illness following the break with his beloved Giulietta Guicciardi. The upshot of this was the "Heiligenstadt Testament."

29. This is Fraülein von Westernholt, about whom more can be found in the editor's "Beethoven's Women Friends" in the *Neue Berliner Musikzeitung* of 1892.

30. In this place there will, of course, be no further examination of Beethoven's love for his Giulietta, to whom the Sonata Fantasia in C Sharp Minor was dedicated. Only one particular passage from this letter should be singled out for special recognition: "This transformation has been brought about by a dear enchanting girl who loves me and whom I love." In no other place did Beethoven write of any woman "who loves me and whom I love."

31. That Beethoven appreciated von Breuning's musical talent, particularly as a violinist, is evident from his dedication of his only Violin Concerto in D (Op. 61) to his friend Stephan v. Breuning.

And his own arrangement of the Violin Concerto for piano was dedicated to Frau von Breuning.

32. Beethoven wished to have the baptismal certificate, because in 1810 he seriously considered marrying. Many suppositions have been offered as to which woman was the object of his marriage plans. I myself believe it was Therese von Malfatti. The details appear in my article "The Malfatti Sisters" (from "Beethoven's Women Friends") in the Sunday Supplement to the *Vossische Zeitung* of February 5 and 12, 1905.

33. These deeply felt song texts in favor of Freemasonry, which Wegeler presents in the appendix to this work, were in any case of his own composition. The Matthisson "Opferlied" (in E) begins with the words: "The flame blazes, wild light shines through the gloomy oak grove." The composition (in C), "Der freie Mann," for choir and solo voices, was written by G.C. Pfeffel and begins: "Who is a free man? Only he whose lawgiver is his own free will and not the tyrant's whim."

34. The variations mentioned here are the Twelve Variations for Piano and Violin in F on the well-known theme "Se vuol ballare" from Mozart's *Figaro*, in the Breitkopf and Härtel edition, series 12, no. 12. The variations were published in 1793 by Artaria under the title assigned by Nottebohm: *XII Variations pour le Clavecin ou Piano-Forte avec un Violon obligé Composées et Dediées à Mademoiselle Eleonore de Breuning par Mr. Beethoven. Oeuvre I.* It is thus especially noteworthy that Beethoven's first compositions to be published in Vienna were not the three Trios (Opus 1) but rather these Variations in F (Oeuvre I). Later this composition was designated as No. 1; the publisher was changed from Artaria to F. Mollo. Compare Wegeler's account above (p. 15) of the "Variations No. 1" dedicated to the woman who was later to become his wife. The second composition dedicated to Eleonore von Breuning, Easy Sonata in C (Fragment) (Breitkopf & Härtel, series 16, no. 36) was first published by Fr. Ph. Dunst in Frankfurt am Main under the title given by Nottebohm: *Sonate pour le Pianoforte Composée et dediée à Mlle. Eleonore de Breuning par L. van Beethoven.* The second movement of this little sonata, or rather, sonatina, is known to have been added to by Ferd. Ries; a third

movement is completely missing. Nottebohm's note in the *Thematic Index:* "Eleonore von Breuning is thought to have received the original manuscript from Beethoven in 1796" (cf. Cäcilia XIII, 284; Wegeler's *Notes*, p. 57) is in any case mistaken. Fraülein von Breuning must have already received the sonatina in Bonn, where the little work must have been composed. This small question is connected with Beethoven's second letter to this lady friend of his youth and will be briefly considered along with it.

35. This is Abbé Gelenik, who lived from 1758 to 1825 and was called the Variations-Smith.

36. Concerning this letter I direct the reader to my articles "Beethoven's Women Friends," published in the *Neue Berliner Zeitung* in 1892, in the second of which Beethoven's relationship with Eleonore von Breuning is considered. This letter is discussed in the issue of June 16, 1892. The key sentence reads: "Everyone unreluctantly accepts that this letter was actually written to Fraülein von Breuning from Vienna; however, everyone will be astonished to learn that I now in all seriousness claim that this undated letter of Beethoven to Eleonore von Breuning was written not in Vienna but rather sent to his pupil and friend from Bonn." The evidence is presented there. Independently of this, Dr. H. Deiters ten years later arrived at the same conclusion, as one reads in the first volume of the second edition of the Thayer-Deiters Beethoven biography. However, I will now add the assertion, already hinted at above, that the sonata mentioned in this letter (Easy Piano Sonata in C) was not, as is claimed, composed around 1796 in Vienna but rather much earlier, in about 1790 or 1791, in Bonn.

37. Stephan von Breuning must have confounded the words "Fidelio" and "Eleonore"; one should examine Otto Jahn's article "Leonore or Fidelio?" in his *Collected Essays on Music* — for which, moreover, A.W. Thayer provided the impetus; see his *Beethoven* II, 301. The theater program appended in Thayer's book actually calls the opera "Fidelio." Also compare the excellent introductory essay by Dr. Erich Prieger to his piano arrangement *Leonore, Opera in Three Acts by Ludwig van Beethoven* (Leipzig, Breitkopf & Härtel, 1905).

37a. Nevertheless, Fidelio did not receive its first performance until nine years later, in Berlin, in October 1815.

38. The date of Ferdinand Ries' arrival in Vienna and at Beethoven's is clearly placed too early. The works named, *Christ on the Mount of Olives* and especially the Second Symphony in D provide the strongest evidence. Autumn 1801 may in fact be considered the time at which F. Ries became Beethoven's pupil. Compare Thayer's detailed exposition in his Beethoven biography (II,63). The Second Symphony was composed in the year 1802 and performed for the first time in April 1803. The oratorio *Christ on the Mount of Olives* was not composed in 1800 — as one might conclude from this and as others, even Nottebohm, assert — but rather in 1801 and revised in 1802; it was first performed in April 1803 in the Theater an der Wien. In general, the chronology in Ries' first account seems quite confused. One should not be too surprised by this, since Ries, as he himself assures us, related things as they had impressed themselves upon his memory: "It should be easy for the reader, if it is of importance to him, to bring some order to this." — Let us, therefore, do our part.

39. This large rehearsal with obligato refreshments at Prince Karl von Lichnowsky's, to whom the Second Symphony is dedicated, must have taken place shortly before April 5, 1803 or on the day of the performance itself (April 5).

40. Actually in 1803.

41. It is not easy to understand how Wegeler can link this delightful anecdote with the composer Paër. *Die schöne Müllerin* (La Molinara) is, of course, an opera by Paisiello. Probably Wegeler confused the composers Paër and Paisiello with one another.

42. Daniel Steibelt was born in Berlin in 1755 (by some accounts in 1765) the son of a piano manufacturer. Beginning at about the age of 30 he created a universal sensation as a piano virtuoso as well as a composer, particularly of chamber works. In Paris he achieved great success with his opera *Romeo and Juliet* with libretto by Viscount de Ségur. Later he became music director in Petersburg, where he died in September 1823. His character both as a person and artist was subjected to diverse bitter criticism. Today only a little is still known

about this rival of Beethoven, who was once highly celebrated in almost all creative fields. Occasionally some of Steibelt's études pop up in étude collections.

43. Giovanni Punto (not Ponto) is the Italianized name of the thoroughly German musician Johann Wenzel Stich, who was born in Czaslau, Bohemia as a serf of Count von Thun. 1775, the year of birth given by Schindler, is probably much too late, since he certainly created a sensation in Paris as early as 1778, where he played a silver horn. He died in Prague in 1803. He had fled from his master with several other musicians. As the story goes, the Count was principally concerned about Stich and had him pursued. The Count is said to have given his bloodhounds the noble commission, in the event that they were unable to gain control over the hornplayer, at least to smash in his front teeth so that he could no longer play the horn. Stich, however, changed his name to Punto and under this appelation attained a high reputation as a virtuoso. When he came to Vienna toward the end of the century, he became friendly with Beethoven, who was particularly fascinated by his life story. For Punto's concerts in 1800 Beethoven wrote the Horn Sonata in F (also to be performed by cello and piano). In manuscript form it may have been dedicated to Stich. However, when the sonata was published in 1801, Baroness von Braun received the dedication. Punto's fellow countrymen honored him in extraordinary fashion. At his funeral the Mozart Requiem was performed. Indeed his grave was adorned with the following Latin distichon:

> Omne tulit punctum Punto, cui Musa Bohemia
> Ut plausit vivo, sic moriente gemit.
>
> (Such praise was won by Punto, who is mourned after
> In death by the Bohemian muse that exulted him in life.)

He wrote numerous works for his instrument.

44. The sonata can probably better be designated as the Sonata in A major, as indeed it usually is.

45. This scene took place during the memorable concert of December 22, 1808. Different witnesses give different accounts, of

which A.W. Thayer has already presented a few versions. A complete summary is to be found in my articles "The Prussian Court Conductor J.F. Reichardt and Beethoven" in the illustrated Berlin weekly *Der Bär* nos. 14-16, of January 7, 14, and 21, 1888. Ferdinand Ries is obviously painting here with overly garish strokes, as can be recognized from the accounts of Reichardt, Czerny, Dolezalek, Moscheles and others presented in these articles.

46. In our time this probably goes without saying. Whoever has had the chance to peruse G. Nottebohm's both scholarly and painstaking book, *Beethoven's Studies: Volume One: Beethoven's Studies with J. Haydn, Albrechtsberger and Salieri* (Leipzig and Winterthur, 1873), must be completely convinced of the truth of von Seyfried's statement.

47. This, however, is in no way evidence against von Seyfried's statement. For one finds parallel fifths not only elsewhere in Beethoven, but in Mozart as well. It would probably not be at all difficult to find so-called "perfect fifths" (that is, major fifths) even in Haydn and in every great master. And yet, no one will contest the assertion that all of our truly great masters have pursued the most assiduous theoretical studies.

48. The first two sonatas of Opus 31, in G and in D minor, were composed in 1802 and first appeared without opus numbers at the beginning of 1803 in the fifth part of the collection *Repertoire des clavecinistes,* published by H.G. Nägeli in Zurich. Soon thereafter they were in fact published by N. Simrock in Bonn under the title *Deux sonates, pour le Pianoforte composées par Louis van Beethoven. Oeuvre 31 . . . Édition très Correcte.* Then, however, they were published again by J. Cappi in Vienna as Opus 29: *Deux Sonates pour le Clavecin ou Piano-Forte, etc.* The third sonata, in E flat, did not appear until 1804, without opus number, in the 11th part of Nägeli's *Repertoire* and in 1805 was included in the Vienna edition. From this it becomes clear that Beethoven's great anger with the tyrannical Nägeli had subsided. Cappi in Vienna published all three sonatas in 1805 under the new title: *Trois Sonates pour le Clavecin ou Piano-Forte composées par Louis van Beethoven. Oeuvre 29* (!) (in Nottebohm's *Thematic Index* p. 35, 2nd ed.) What still does not cease to astonish is the fact that such a pro-

found, extensive three-part set of sonatas was published without a dedication.

49. They were published in March 1804 by the Bureau d'Art et d'Industrie.

50. Who this young count may have been cannot be traced with certainty. L. Nohl interprets the P. . . . as Count "Palffy," thereby evoking a polemic from Thayer (Thayer II, 201). But Thayer's argument that the number of dots does not fit with "Palffy" with two "f's" is not very sound, for Ries may very well have written this name with one "f" and have thought of it that way.

51. This may very well signify Princess (Josephine von) Liechtenstein, Landgravine of Fürstenberg, to whom the Sonata in E-flat major, Opus 27, No. 1 (March 1802) is dedicated.

52. In the beginning of 1803.

52a. This judgment is, however, very much in need of qualification, as can be inferred particularly from a Beethoven letter dated July 13, 1802 to Breitkopf & Härtel. See the editor's *Beethoven's Complete Letters,* no. 53, and the accompanying notes.

53. These matters belong in the period of Ferdinand Ries's second stay in Vienna. The story of the Kappellmeister position in Cassel belongs in the year 1809.

54. This may have been in 1804. The sonata itself was not published until February 1807.

55. This is August Alexander Klengel, who later became so famous as a contrapuntist; born 1784 in Dresden, died there 1852. His chief work, *Canons et Fugues dan tous les tons majeurs et mineurs pour le Piano*, was published after Klengel's death in 1854 by Moritz Hauptmann through Breitkopf & Härtel. — "At the Swan" refers to the tavern Beethoven so loved to patronize, known variously as *zum Schwan, Schwann, von der Schwann, im Schwann* and *zur Schwann*. It plays a considerable role in his letters to von Zmeskall.

56. This deservedly beloved composition, known under the name "Andante favori," was composed in 1804 and published in May 1806 with the title *Andante pour le Pianoforte compose par Louis van Beethoven*. See also the explanatory note to letter no. 83 (to

Ferdinand Ries) in *Beethoven's Complete Letters.*

57. This is Wenzel Krumpholz, the famous violinist, under whose guidance Beethoven further improved his skills on the violin. On May 2, 1817 he died suddenly on the Promenade. On the day immediately following Beethoven memorialized this most devoted friend with the "Song of the Monks" from Schiller's *Wilhelm Tell* ("Suddenly death comes to man," etc.), written in Aloys Fuchs' family album.

58. Not 1807 but rather 1806.

59. This in turn belongs at the end of 1808, when Beethoven gave the December 22 academy concert already mentioned above, during which the drastic incident described by Ries, Spohr, Reichardt and others took place. Anna Milder, however, did not sing the aria intended for her at that time, for as a consequence of a quarrel between Beethoven and Hauptmann, her future husband, she was not allowed to participate in the concert and was replaced by Schuppanzigh's sister-in-law, Josephine Killitschky, later the wife of Counselor-at-Law Schulze. — Nanette Marconi, the future Frau Schönberger, whom Beethoven also considered on this occasion, was an outstanding contralto from Mannheim.

60. The great Sonata for the Hammerklavier in B was composed in part in 1818 in Mödling. It was published by Artaria in Vienna, in September 1819.

61. A more detailed and accurate account of this is presented in the editor's article "Beethoven in Berlin" (*Nord und Süd*, November 1886).

62. Compare with note 27.

63. In von Seyfried's *Ludwig van Beethoven's Studies,* second edition, appendix, page 10.

64. The C Minor Concerto (Opus 37), dedicated to Prince Louis Ferdinand of Prussia, had already been composed in 1800, before Ferdinand Ries was even Beethoven's student in Vienna. The C Minor Concerto was performed in Beethoven's academy concert of April 5, 1803, at a time when Prince Louis Ferdinand was most probably in Vienna. It was not published until November 1804. It

does not appear, however, that Ries meant precisely this academy concert, because, according to the account of this concert, Beethoven himself was the pianist in the C Minor Concerto.

65. The Concerto in G was ready for the printer in 1807. It was published by the Industriekomtoir in August 1808, with a dedication to Archduke Rudolf.

65a. The theater is called the Kärnthner-Thor Theater.

66. Compare with note 57.

66a. A. & Company = Artaria and Company. Compare Beethoven's stinging letter to Breitkopf & Härtel on the Quintet, which was published for the first time in the editor's *Beethoven's Complete Letters*, (no. 60, of November 13, 1802, with explanatory notes).

67. These were certainly the Twelve Variations in A on the Russian Dance from the Ballet "The Maid of the Forest" by P. Wranitzky, dedicated to Countess von Browne.

67a. Beethoven found himself in an irresolute state of mind when it appeared necessary to find someone to whom to dedicate the Diabelli Variations. At this time Beethoven felt himself beholden not only to Frau Antonia Brentano but also to his friend Ries, then living in London. He vacillated back and forth until the scale tilted more and more in favor of his Frankfurt friend. In Schindler's collection of Beethoven's posthumous papers in the Royal Library in Berlin there is a particularly small scrap of paper on which is written in Beethoven's hand in a lapidary style: "The dedication of the two sonatas in A Sharp and C Minor is to Frau Brentano, born Edle von Birkenstock. — Ries — nothing." Certainly new material for resentment of Ries had accumulated and to him was dedicated neither one of these sonatas nor even the variations; nor to his wife. One of the consequences of this irresolution may have been the fact that Opus 110 and Opus 111 received no dedication at all. For even the dedication of Opus 111 to the Archduke Rudolf did not derive from Beethoven himself but rather from the publisher.

68. It was not the Andante con Variazioni but rather the so-called Andante Favori in F that was composed in 1804 and published in 1806.

68a. Because of his stoutness Schuppanzigh received the nickname "Mylord Falstaff" from Beethoven. In two canons Beethoven's sense of humor glorifies Schuppanzigh's corpulence.

69. The dead friend was probably Lenz (Lorenz) von Breuning, who had already died in 1798 in Bonn; the other, perhaps Pastor Karl Amenda of Kurland or even Franz Wegeler.

70. The name Salomon can probably only bring to mind the violinist Johann Peter Salomon, who was born about 1745 in Bonn. When in later years he chose London as his place of residence, he did a great deal for German music. In 1790 he prevailed upon Haydn to travel to England. He was also frequently in communication with Beethoven. It is now well known that in August 1815 he suffered a calamitous fall from a horse, dying from the effects of that fall in November of the same year. The above letter from Beethoven to Ries was, as we see, written on November 22, 1815. Thus one can only assume that either Beethoven on this day knew nothing of Salomon's death or that Salomon did not die until after November 22, 1815. Compare this with Beethoven's letter of February 28, 1816, in which maestro Salomon's death is painfully lamented.

71. The two-hands piano arrangement of the A major Symphony, dedicated to Empress Elisabeth Alexiewna, is not by Beethoven himself but merely corrected by him. The violin sonata here named is Opus 96 in G, which was completed at the end of 1812. It was published by S.A. Steiner & Company in Vienna in July 1816 along with the Trio in B flat, Opus 97. The latter had already been composed in March 1811, was not given to the engraver until June 1816, and was published on July 16, 1816. With the trio Beethoven made his last public appearances as a pianist: on April 11, 1814, and some weeks later in one of Schuppanzigh's morning concerts in the Prater.

72. A most curious utterance: "I found only one, whom I will most likely never possess." Who may this woman have been? In all likelihood it was Amalie Sebald, later Frau Justizrat Krause, with whom Beethoven had been quite taken for some years. In this same year he expressed himself in a similar vein to the Giannatasio del Rio family when they visited him in Baden in the company of his

nephew. Beethoven said of himself that he had loved unluckily. Five years ago he had become acquainted with a woman, and it would have been the greatest joy of his life to have bound himself more closely to her. It wasn't to be thought of, a near impossibility, a chimera; however it was now just as on the first day. He had still not found this harmony. However, it could not be explained; he still could not put it out of his mind. And all that had been inflicted upon him by the dark-eyed Amalie Sebald.

73. This letter of Beethoven to F. Ries is presented here in only fragmentary form. I had the opportunity to become acquainted with this letter, which is in the possession of an offspring of the Ries family, namely the Berlin composer and music publisher Franz Ries, and was granted permission to copy it with a view to using it. The original manuscript of this letter must also have been available to Herr A.W. Thayer, who published it in its complete form in his Beethoven biography (III,395f), without, of course, mentioning anything about his copy. Here it is intended only to indicate the variant and missing passages in the footnotes. First: Vienna with "v", as often with Beethoven. Orthographic matters will otherwise be overlooked.

74. [Indication of a variant in the German text.]

75. Here the following portion is missing: "In any case I must ask you to apply to H. Birshall for the 10 ducats and to make sure that you yourself get them. I guarantee you on my honor that I have already paid 21 florins for expenses and that is without taking into account the copyist's charges and several postal fees in bank notes. The money was not even sent to me in ducats, although you yourself had written that it was to be sent to me in Dutch ducats. — Are there also in England such conscientious persons who put no value on keeping their word?" — [On the second page are the following words, written on the side]: "NB did you dedicate your Concerto in E flat to Archduke Rudolf? Why did you not write to him yourself about it?" — "With regard to the Trio the publisher here in Vienna has suggested to me that this be published in London on the last day of August. Therefore, I beg you to be so kind as to speak to Herr B. about it. Herr B. can make preparations for the piano arrangement

of the Symphony in A, for I will let you or Herr B. know as soon as the publisher here names the day."

76. Here the following words are omitted: "since his arrival in L."

77. [Indication of a variant in the German text.]

78. In the original: "the quartet."

79. The following words are omitted: "because I also wish to publish it here soon, and what I have to expect with regard to the Cello Sonatas?" The quartet in question here is the Quartet in F Minor, Opus 95, written in 1810 and published in December 1816; the cello sonatas mentioned here are those in C and D (Opus 102), composed in 1815 and published in 1817 in Bonn.

80-82. [Indication of a variant in the German text.]

83. In the original: "Morning cronigle."

84. [Indication of a variant in the German text.]

85. In the original: "by N."

86. The material in parentheses is missing in the original text.

87-88. [Indication of a variant in the German text.]

89. This concluding passage is omitted by Ries: "The piano arrangement of the Symphony in A was copied rapidly, and after a more thorough review I have had the copies changed in some places, of which I will inform you. My best to your wife. In haste, your true friend, Beethoven."

This letter takes up four quarto sheets, three of which are completely covered with writing. There is no envelope. The address on the fourth page — not in Beethoven's hand — reads: "Mr. Ferd. Ries, in care of Mr. B.A. Goldschmid, London" — without street name or number.

90. This is Cypriani Potter, pianist and composer, born in London in 1792; he became director of the Royal Academy of Music there in 1825 and died in London in September 1872. In his travels he had become acquainted with Beethoven in Vienna.

91. The three overtures are: a) to A. von Kotzebue's "Ruins of Athens," which was performed for the first time in February 1812

and published in February 1823; b) the Overture in C, Op. 115, dedicated to the Princess von Radziwill, also called the Name Day [Zur Namensfeier] Overture; it was given its first performance on December 25, 1815. And this overture, which Beethoven at its publication in 1825 characterized — uniquely — as "composed for large orchestra," found no favor with the English, who were otherwise such Beethoven enthusiasts! c) The Overture in E-flat to von Kotzebue's prologue "Hungary's First Benefactor, King Stephan" (Op. 117); it received its first performance in February 1812 along with the *Ruins of Athens* Overture. This overture, as beautiful as it is original, had been given to the publisher in 1815 but was not published until July 1826; it was characterized by Beethoven as a "Grand Overture."

92. The quintet for string instruments (C minor) named here was arranged by Beethoven himself from his C Minor Trio (Opus 1) and received the opus number 104. As is well known, Beethoven wrote at the head of the manuscript: "Trio arranged as a four-voiced quintet by Mr. Goodwill, brought into the daylight by the radiance of five voices, and raised from great misery to considerable respect by Mr. Benevolence. Vienna, August 14, 1817. NB: The original three part quintet score is presented to the lower gods as a solemn burnt offering." Performed on December 10, 1818 in Vienna, the Quintet in C Minor was published in February 1819. See also the editor's *New Beethoven Letters*, page 31.

93. The great Sonata in B-flat (Op. 106), the subject of this and the following letter, was actually published in September 1819.

94. The second movement of this gigantic sonata later received the marking *Scherzo assai vivace.* The metronome reading is 𝅗𝅥. = 80, not 𝅗𝅥 = 80. The introduction to the great concluding fugue now reads *Largo.* However, one should not overlook the statement in the following letter to Ries: "The sonata was written under oppressive circumstances." What a triumph of pure genius!

95. The great *Missa Solemnis* in D (Opus 123) had already been started in 1818 but was not completely finished until March 1823.

96. Beethoven may now indeed have seriously considered hon-

oring with a dedication the friend and pupil who had been of such assistance to him.

97. It was the city of Boston which at about this time gave instructions to commission from Beethoven an oratorio for its music society — this, however, produced no positive results.

97a. Beethoven is most likely once more speaking of the charming Potter, whom he had already earlier called Botter; therefore, to be correct this should read P. and not B. — Despite these terrible times his divine sense of humor did not desert him. This is how one must grasp the numerous jokes about Ries' beautiful wife. — The Ninth Symphony was, however, later directed to another address, that of Frederick William III, King of Prussia.

98. These are the eleven (or twelve) new Bagatelles for Piano, published as Opus 119.

99. It is the Overture in C (Opus 124), *The Consecration of the House,* dedicated to the Princess von Galitzin. It was performed at the opening of the Josephstadt Theater on October 3, 1822 and was published in 1825 by B. Schott's Sons in Mainz.

100. It is the *Opferlied,* Opus 121b (text by Matthisson — "The flame blazes" —), which according to Schindler's information (II,152), Beethoven composed for a solo voice with choir and orchestra for Prof. Ehler's benefit concert in Pressburg in 1822. This is an arrangement of a much earlier song composed on the same text. The earlier song "The flame blazes" in E was certainly composed before 1800.

101. The Overture in C already mentioned (Op. 115, *Zur Namensfeier*) also known as the "Hunt Overture." This "poetic" overture was published in 1825.

102. The impressive overture *The Consecration of the House*, Opus 124, also in C.

103. During the years of his lengthy guardianship litigation, Beethoven had ample opportunity to concern himself with his "van." One of the *Conversation Books* from 1819 (notebook no. 30, leaf 42a) contains the following remarks in Beethoven's hand concerning the word "van": "Van indicates nobility and patrician status

only (42b) when it stands in the middle between two proper names [i.e. family names], e.g. Bantink van Dieperheim (Halt van Strenloo [or Streelang]). One would get the best information on this insignificant significance from the Dutch."

104. The nephew, Karl van Beethoven, died as a respected citizen in 1858.

105. However, it is an established fact that Beethoven certainly concerned himself with extracts from Kant's philosophy. Particularly Kantian moral philosophy, with its categorical imperative, seemed to have been written as if from his inmost thoughts. Bearing witness to this are passages in the *Conversation Books*, for example in number 22 from Spring 1820, where Beethoven himself recorded in lapidarian hand (leaf 17a): "The moral law within us, and the starry sky above us. — Kant!!!"

106. Mention of Beethoven's finger infection is also made in a recently released letter from this time in which the composer writes: "My colic is better, but yesterday my poor finger had to undergo a serious nail operation. When I wrote to you yesterday it looked very threatening. Today it is quite limp with pain." (*New Beethoven Letters*, p. 38).

107. In 1823, just as he was composing the Ninth Symphony, Beethoven suffered from a serious eye disease, traces of which lingered until the beginning of 1824. See the editor's detailed treatise "Beethoven's Eyes and Eyelids" in the first Beethoven issue of *Musik* (1903).

108. The name of this ill-famed man was Dr. *Wawruch*.

109-112. [References are to page numbers in Kalischer's edition.]

113. These words of Rellstat resulted from his visit to Beethoven in 1825. All of this as well as everything else concerned with Mozart and Beethoven is exhaustively detailed in the editor's article "Beethoven's Connections with Mozart," in the first Mozart issue of *Musik* (October 1904).

114. The editor should not like to leave unmentioned that he has scrutinized many volumes of the memoirs of the Marquise von

Abrantes (the wife of General von Junot) without finding this statement or anything else from her pen dealing with Beethoven. Dr. Wegeler must have owned a very special edition. I would be very grateful to anyone who could assist me in locating these words in the original.

115-119. [References are to page numbers in Kalischer's edition.]

120. This passage with its terse manner of expression offers further evidence of Beethoven's acquaintance with Kant's works; it appears to me to be reminiscent of Kant's *Anthropology*.

121. This is confirmed by A. Schindler. It was J.A. Stumpf, the German-English Beethoven enthusiast, who in 1826 presented Beethoven with the complete works of Handel in 40 folio volumes. The composer's pleasure at this was infinitely great (see Schindler, II, 139, note).

122. See note 123.

123. These verses are by Schiller — a fact which I discovered quite by chance only a few years ago. They are from *Don Carlos*, the speech of Marquis Posa to the Queen in Act 4, scene 21.

124. [The reference is to the page number in Kalischer's edition.]

125. The name of the librettist is Soulié. However, the song had already been published as a supplement to the *Leipziger Allgemeine Musikalische Zeitung* of November 22, 1809 with the title *Als die Geliebte sich trennen wollte*. For further information on this see Nottebohm, *Thematic Index*, p. 179 (1868).

Index

Entries preceded by the letter "k" refer to the number of the note by A. C. Kalischer. These notes are indicated by bold superscripts in the text, and begin after the text, on page 168. Index entries in bold type refer to illustrations.

Albrechtsberger, Johann Georg 75
Apponyi, Count Anton Georg 33
Artaria and Co. (publisher) 30, 107, 113, k34, k60, k66a

Bach, Johann Sebastian 33, 73, 153
Baden 79, 116, 117, k72
Baums, Gertrude (godmother) 9, 11
Beethoven, Caspar Anton Carl van (brother) 12, 76-77, 82, 104, 112, 121, 123, k22
Beethoven, Johann van (father) 7, 13-14, 109, ***110***, 148, k3
Beethoven, Karl van (nephew) 123, ***124***, 147, k7, k22, k72, k104
Beethoven, Ludwig van (grandfather) 7, 12-14
Beethoven, Ludwig van
- Birth and family history 7-12, 46, 146-147, k2, k3, k4-k8, k103
- Characteristics
    - absentmindedness of 86-87, 107-108
    - appearance of 14
    - clumsiness of 106
    - generosity of 28, 114, 121-122, 132
    - temperament of 34-35, 52, 67, 71, 73, 76, 80, 83-85, 88-90, 102, 108, 116-119, k20, k22, k45, k48, k59
    - Diplomas and honors 49, 97
- Education, general 14, 148
- Education, music
    - organ playing 17-18, k11, k12, k12a
    - teachers 14, 17, 75, 106, k10, k11, k12
- Finances 28, 36-38, 59, 84, 100, 109, 110, 121-126, 131-132, 133-135, 137, k75
- Health
    - deafness 26, 28-29, 40, 45, 86-87
    - illnesses 40-41, 51, 132, k26, k28, k106, k107

Beethoven, Ludwig van (continued)
Music
composing 17, 22, 25, 54, 65-67, 71-72, 76, 80, 87-88, 92, 95, k16, k34, k107
conducting 66, 73, 102, k45
improvisation 21, 25, 68, 71, 87-88, 97
performing
chamber musician, as 21, 32, 69
organist, as 18, 20, k12a
pianist, as 23, 25, 32, 34, 54, 70-71, 80-82, 94, k24
violinist, as 106, k31, k57
Portraits ***frontispiece***, ***viii***, 30, ***47***, 50, 51, 124, 129, ***160***-161
Relationships
von Breunings 14-16, k1, k31
enemies and rivals 56, 59, 70-71, 83, 88-89, 97-98, k42, k55
guardian, as 123-124, 134, k103
parents, to 13-14, 24, 109, 147
women, with 41, 43, 52, 104-105, 124, k28, k30, k32, k34, k36, k72
Residences 11, ***12***, 30, 66, 79, 100, 116-117, ***147***, k27
Teacher, as 14, 24, 80, 82, 83
Travels, 23-24, 96,155-156

Beethoven, Ludwig Maria van (older brother) 9, 46
Beethoven, Maria Magdalena Kewerich (mother) 7-9, 13, 49, 109, k3
Beethoven, Nicolaus Johannes 12, 83, 85, 116, 138, ***139***
Belderbusch, Countess Barbara (née Koch) 55
Bernhard, Karl k9
Berlin 60-94, k9, k37a, k42, k61
Bonaparte, Napoleon 57, 68
Bonn 4-5, 31, k1, k2, k4, k7, k10, k16, k34, k36, k48, k69, k70
Boosey and Co. (publishers) 110, 138
Brentano, Frau Antonie von k67a
Breuning, Christoph von 15, 30, 39, 155
Breuning, Eleonore Brigitte von xii, 15, 31, 48, 50, 52-54, 56-57, k34, k36
Breuning, family von ***15***, ***16***, 24-25, 30-31, 48, 50, 53, 56, 57, k1, k20
Breuning, Frau Helene von 15-16, 24, 31, 39, 42, 56, k31
Breuning, Gerhard von 158, 162
Breuning, Lenz von 15, 156, k69
Breuning, Stephan von xiv, 5, 15-16, **30**, 42-45, 50-51, 77, 86, 91, 100, 116-119, 155-156, 159-163, k31, k37

Bridgetower, George Augustus 72
Browne-Camus, Count Johann Georg von 79-80, 104
Browne-Camus, Countess Anna Margarette von k67

Clementi and Co. (publishers) 110
Clementi, Muzio 88-89
Cologne 7, 9, 18
Coutts and Co. (bankers) 121, 122
Cramer, Johann Baptist 87, 128
Czerny, Carl 157, k45

Döbling (residence) 86-87, 100, 117
Dunst (publisher) 22, 54, 93, k34
Duport, Pierre (cellist) 97

Eeden, Heinrich van den [van der Eden] 17, k11
Esterhazy, Prince Paul 129
Esterhazy, Princess Marie 80

Förster, Emmanuel Aloys 34
Friedrich Wilhelm II, King of Prussia 10, 48, 96, k9
Friedrich Wilhelm III, King of Prussia k97a
Fries, Count Moritz von 71

Gelinek, Abbé Joseph 57, k35
George IV, King of England 95-96, 136
Giucciardi, Giulietta k28, k30
Goethe, Johann Wolfgang von 39

Handel, Georg Friedrich 73, 153, 155, 158, k121,
Hatzfeld, Countess Maria von 22
Haydn, Franz Joseph 22, 32, 67, 74-75, 113, k13, k46, k47, k70
Heiligenstadt 66, **67**, k28
Heller, Ferdinand 20
Himmel, Friedrich Heinrich **97**-98
Hogarth, William 104, 109
d'Honrath, Jeanette 42

Kant, Immanuel 148, k105, k120
Kärnthner-Thor Theater 102, k65a
Kewerich, Heinrich (maternal grandfather) 9, k3, k4
Kewerich, Maria Westorffs (maternal grandmother) 8, k3, k4
Kinsky, Prince Ferdinand Johann Nepomuk 84

Kirnberger, Johann Phillip 64
Klengel, August Alexander 88, k55
Kraft, Anton 32, k19
Kraft, Nikolaus 32, k19
Krumpholz, Wenzel 89, k57

Lichnowsky, Prince Karl 27, 32-36, 60, 66, 70, 74, 89-91, **92**, 103, k19, k39
Lichnowsky, Princess Maria Christiane 34, 91, **92**
Lichnowsky Quartet 32, k19
Liechtenstein, Princess Josephine Sophia von 81-82, 120, k51
Linke, Joseph 32, k19
Lobkowitz, Prince Franz Joseph von 67, 84, k19
London Philharmonic Society 124, 126-129, 138
Louis Ferdinand, Prince of Prussia 98-99, k64

Malchus, , Karl August von 53, 55, 152
Malfatti, Therese von k32
Matthisson, Friedrich von (poet) 46, 61, k33, k100
Maximilian Franz, Archduke (Elector of Cologne) 17-18, **56**
Maximilian Friedrich (Elector of Cologne) 13
Mayer [Meyer], Sebastian 92
Mölker-Bastei (residence) 30, 39, 100, k27
Mozart, Wolfgang Amadeus 54, 73, 75, 153, 155, k1, k17, k34, k43, k47, k113
Music
    Arrangements 68, k15, k28, k37, k71, k75, k89, k92, k100
    Manuscripts 100-101, 111-112
    Posthumous publications 111-112
    Works *see separate Index of Musical Compositions*

Nageli, Hans Georg (publisher) 76-77
Neate, Charles 125-126, 127-129, 133
Neefe, Christian Gottlob 17, ***18***, 14n, k10, k12

Oberdöbling (residence) 115
Odescalchi, Princess Barbara (neé Keglevics) 82, k24

Paer, Ferdinando 70, k41
Paisiello, Giovanni k41
Palffy, Count Ferdinand 80, k50
Paraquin, Johann Baptist 57
Pasqualati [Pasquillati] house (residence) 100, k27
Pfeiffer, Tobias 17, k11

Pleyel, Ignaz Joseph 21, k13
Potter [Botter], Cipriani 128, k90, k97a
Publishers 76-79, 82, 107, 113, 129, 138, k48
Punto [Ponto], Giovanni *see* Stich, Johann Wenzel

Ram, Friedrich 69
Razumovsky, Count Andreas k19
Reichardt, Johann Friedrich 84, k45, k59
Ries, Ferdinand *Introduction*, 1-3, 26, 31, **63**-64, 79-90, 101-106, ***142***, k17, k34, k38, k53, k56, k64, k67a, k97a
Ries, Franz (father of author) xix, 13, 21, 23, 26, 31, 44, 65, 82, 103
Röckel, Joseph August 93
Romberg, Andreas 23, 55
Romberg, Bernhard 21, 23, 55, k13
Rudolph, Johann Joseph Rainier, Archduke 84, **99**, 101, 125, 132, 136

Salieri, Antonio 75, k46
Salomon, Johann Peter 122, 123, k70
Schindler, Anton xiv-xix, ***xv***, k18, k19, k24, k43, k67a, k100, k121
Schmidt, Dr. Johann Adam 40, k28
Schuppanzigh, Ignaz 32, 116, k19, k68a
Seyfried, Ignaz Ritter von 14, 17, 37, 38, 42, 75, 85, k12a, k23, k26, k46, k47, k63
Simrock, Nikolaus 23, 77, ***78***, 163, k48
Smart, Sir George 127-128
Steibelt, Daniel 70-71, k42
Sterkel, Abbé 23
Stich, Johann Wenzel [also Ponto or Punto] 71, k43

Theater-an-der-Wien 65, 72, 78, 100, 117

Vering, Dr. Gerhard Ritter von 28, 44
Vogler, Abbé Georg Joseph 17

Waldstein, Count Ferdinand Ernst von ***19***, 20-21, 22, 89
Wegeler, Dr. Franz Gerhard *Introduction*, ***1***, 4-6, 16, 25, 27, 48, 51, 59, 63, k1, k4, k20, k33, k69
Weiss, Franz 32, k19, k43

Zmeskall von Domanovecz, Nikolaus 32, k55

Index of Musical Compositions

Entries preceded by the letter "k" refer to the number of the note by A. C. Kalischer. These notes are indicated by bold superscripts in the text, and begin after the text, on page 168.

Orchestral Music

Symphonies

No.2 in D (Opus 36) 66-67, k38, k39
No.3 in E-flat (Opus 55) 67
No.5 in C minor (Opus 67) 72
No.6 in F (Opus 68) 72
No.7 in A (Opus 92) 121-122, 126, k71, k75, k89
No.9 in D minor (Opus 125) 135, 136, 139, k97a, k107
Wellington's Victory (Battle of Vittoria) (Opus 91) 95-96, 124, 126, 135, 136

Piano Concertos

No.1 in C (Opus 15) 38, 94, k24
No.3 in C minor (Opus 37) 66, 101-103, k64
No.4 in G (Opus 58) 102-103, k65
No.5 in E-flat (Opus 73) 121-122, k71, k75

Other Concertos

Violin (Opus 61) 82, 118, k31

Overtures & Miscellaneous

Consecration of the House (Opus 124) 138, 139, k99, k102
King Stephan (Opus 117) 129, k91
Ritterballet (WoO 1) 22, k15
Ruins of Athens (Opus 113) 112, 129, 139-140, k91
Zur Namensfeier (Opus 115) 129, 140, k91, k101

Chamber Music

Sonatas

Piano and Cello in C and D minor (Opus 102) 125, k79
Piano and Horn (Opus 17) 71, k43
Piano and Violin in A minor (Opus 23) 81-82, k44
Piano and Violin in A (Kreuzer, Opus 47) 72, 115, k68
Piano and Violin in G (Opus 96) 121-122, k71
Variations for Piano and Violin on Mozart's "Se vuol ballare" ("Variations No. 1", WoO 40) 15, 54, 57, k34

Trios

Piano, Clarinet and Cello in B-flat (Opus 11) 70
Piano, Violin and Cello (Opus 1, Nos. 1-3) 32, 74
Piano, Violin and Cello in B-flat (Archduke, Opus 97) 121-122, k71, k75
String Trio (Opus 3) 33

String Quartets

Opus 18, No.1 (F major) 91
Opus 18, No. 3 (D) 91
Opus 18, No.4 (C minor) 76-77
Opus 95 (F minor) 125, k78, k79
Opus 104 (C minor [arrangement of Opus 1 No.3]) 129, k92
Opus 127 (E-flat) k19
Opus 132 (A minor) k19

Other

Quintet for Piano and Wind Instruments (Opus 16) 69
Septet (Opus 20) 82, k28
String Quintet in C (Opus 29) 107, k66a
String Quintet in E-flat (Opus 4 [revision of Opus 103]) 26

Keyboard Music

Sonatas

Opus 2, Nos. 1-3 (F minor, A, and C) 112-113
Opus 13 (C minor, Pathetique) 94
Opus 26 (A-flat) 70
Opus 27, No.1 (E-flat) k30, k51
Opus 27, No.2 (C-sharp minor, Moonlight) k30, k51
Opus 31, Nos. 1-3 (G, D minor and E-flat) 76, 81, k48
Opus 53 (C, Waldstein) 89-90
Opus 57 (F minor, Appassionata) 87
Opus 106 (B, Hammerclavier) 94-95, 129-131, k60, k93
Opus 110 (A-flat) 110
Opus 111 (C minor) 110
WoO 47 (E-flat, F minor, and D, Electoral) 22
WoO 51 (C) 55, k34, k36

Miscelllaneous

Andante in F (WoO 57) 89, k56, k68
Eleven Bagatelles for Piano (Opus 119) 137, k98
Marches for Four Hands (Opus 45) 80
Variations in F major (Opus 34) 82-83
Variations on "Nel cuor più non mi sento" (WoO 70) 70

Variations on "Vieni amore" (WoO 65) 22-23
Variations on a Russian Dance (WoO 71) 107, k67
Variations on a Waltz by Diabelli (Opus 120) 110, 136-137, k67a

Vocal Music

Cantata on the Death of Emperor Joseph II (WoO 87) 22, k14
Cantata on the Elevation of Leopold II (WoO 88) 22, k14
Christ on the Mount of Olives (Opus 85) 65, k38
Fantasia for Piano, Chorus and Orchestra in C minor ("Choral Fantasy", Opus 80) 72-73
Fidelio (Opus 72) 58-60, 90-93, k37, k37a
Missa Solemnis in D (Opus 123) 133, 140, k95

Songs

"Als die Geliebte sich trennen wollte" ("Empfindungen bei Lydiens Untreue", WoO 132) 163-165, k125
"Der freie Mann" ("Wer ist ein freier Mann?", WoO 117) 46, 61, k33
"Die Klage" (WoO 113) 62, 143
"Opferlied" (Opus 121b) 61, 140, k33, k100,
"Wenn jemand eine Reise thut" (Opus 52, No.1) 22